Thomas M. Cooley.

Eng^d by E. G. Williams & Bro. New York

TO WIT:

DEPARTMENT OF LAW

UNIVERSITY OF MICHIGAN

CLASS OF '94

Lex est ab Æterno

FOUNDED AND PUBLISHED
BY THE
SENIOR LAW CLASS OF '94

THE REGISTER PUBLISHING CO.

TO THE MEMORY OF THE LATE

CHRISTIAN H. BUHL,

WHOSE LIBERAL BENEFACTIONS TO THE DEPARTMENT

OF LAW OF THE UNIVERSITY OF MICHIGAN, HAVE

GREATLY FACILITATED THE STUDY OF LAW

AT THIS INSTITUTION, THIS VOLUME

IS RESPECTFULLY DEDICATED.

BOARD of EDITORS
5.
CHARLES A. DENISON,
EDITOR-IN-CHIEF.
6 EARL D. BABST,
MANAGING EDITOR.
4. OREON E. SCOTT,
BUSINESS MANAGER.
1. EDWIN W. SIMS,
7. EUGENE BATAVIA,
3. G. W. FULLER,
9. HENRY C. WALTERS,
2. CHARLES A. PARK.
DEAN JEROME C. KNOWLTON,
PROF. BRADLEY M. THOMPSON,
PROF. FLOYD R. MECHEM,
ADVISORY BOARD.
8. B. F. WOLLMAN,
10. FRANZ C. KUHN,
ASS'T. BUSINESS MANAGERS.

Resident Graduate Law Class.

Officers.

Chas. K. Friedman,	*President.*
Miss M. E. Benson,	*Vice-President.*
Frank L. Bowen,	*Secretary.*
Wm. C. Swan,	*Treasurer.*
Frank G. Jones,	*Orator.*
Isaac B. Lipson,	*Valedictorian.*
J. Henry Van Tassel,	*Historian.*
Wm. T. Webb,	*Prophet.*
Herbert A. Wright,	*Poet.*

Resident Graduate Law Class and Residence.

Members.

Miss M. E. Benson, LL. B.,	Milwaukee, Wis.
Frank L. Bowen, LL. B.,	Grand Rapids, Mich.
Chas. K. Friedman, LL. B.,	Toledo, Ohio.
Franklin J. Griffen, LL. B.,	Omaha, Neb.
Lloyd F. Harms, LL. B.,	Port Clinton, Ohio.
Jas. S. Henton, LL. B.,	El Paso, Tex.
Robt. A. Howard, LL. B.,	Ann Arbor, Mich.
John B. Hoy, LL. B.,	Joliet, Ills.
Francis G. Jones, LL. B.,	Crystal Lake, Ill.
Isaac B. Lipson, LL. B.,	Leavenworth, Kan.
Fred P. Muhlhauser, LL. B., Cincinnati Law College,	Cincinnati, Ohio.
Stephen A. Nowlin, LL. B.,	Grattan, Mich.

Purcell Rowe, LL. B., ...	Ann Arbor, Mich.
Fritz Rudin, LL. B., ...	Elyria, Ohio.
Oscar F. Sessinghaus, LL. B., ...	St. Louis, Mo.
Chas. W. Scrutchin, LL. B., ...	Detroit, Mich.
Wm. C. Swan, LL. B., Somerset Bridge, .	Bermuda Islands.
J. Henry Van Tassel, LL. B., ...	Ann Arbor, Mich.
Wm. S. Withers, A. B., Univ. of Virg., LL. B., Cumberland Univ., ...	Hopkinsville, Ky.
Herbert A. Wright, B. S., N. Ind. Normal, LL. B., N. Ind. Law College, . . .	Valparasso, Ind.
Wm. T. Webb, LL. B., ...	Williamston, Mich.

Senior Class.

Individual Records.

NED ABERCROMBIE, Δ T Δ, Δ X, ... RUSHVILLE, IND.

One year man. Born at Rushville, Indiana, December 3, 1872. Graduated from Rushville High School. Attended Hanover College, 1889–90. Took Junior year of Law at De Pauw University, 1892–93. At Michigan, member of Indiana Club Court. Expects to practice in Indiana. Permanent address, Rushville, Indiana.

CHARLES FRANCIS ADAMS, ... OLMSTED FALLS, OHIO.

Attended Ada Normal School, Ada, Ohio. Republican. Permanent address, Olmsted Falls, Ohio.

JAMES MORRIS ADAMS, ... FREDONIA, NEW YORK.

Attorney-at-law, Michigan. Born at Dunkirk, New York, September 21, 1869. Attended Fredonia State Normal School. Before entering Michigan, chief clerk in office of L. S. & M. S. R. R. at Dunkirk, New York. At Michigan: Judge of Empire State Practice Court; member of Webster Society. Expects to practice in New York State. Democrat. Permanent address, Fredonia, New York.

JACOB BLACK ADAMS, ... WAYNESBURG, PENN.

B. A. Waynesburg College, 1885. Attorney-at-Law, Pennsylvania, Kansas. One year man. Born at Waynesburg, Greene County, Pennsylvania, 1863. Graduated from Waynesburg College, Class of '85. Before entering Michigan: Practiced law at Springfield, Kansas, 1885–91; District Attorney of Seward County, Kansas, 1889-91; President of Bank of Mansfield, Mansfield, Missouri, 1891–93. At Michigan, Member of Pennsylvania Club Court. Expects to practice at Waynesburg, Greene County, Pennsylvania. Republican. Permanent address, Waynesburg, Pennsylvania.

FREDERIC WILLIAM ASHTON, Δ T Δ, ... BRYON, OHIO.

B. S. Michigan Agricultural College, 1891. Born at Bryon, Ohio, February 22, 1871. Graduated from Bryon High School. Graduated from Michigan Agricultural College, class of '91. At M. A. C., President of Athletic Association. Expects to practice in Kearney, Nebraska. Democrat. Permanent address. Bryon, Ohio.

FERGUS LINCOLN ANDERSON, ... OHIO, ILLINOIS.

One year man. Born at Ohio, Illinois, March 16, 1865. Graduated from Business Institute Valparaiso, Indiana, Normal School, Class of '82. In railroad pursuits 1882–92. Train Dispatcher C. M. & St. P. R. R., Marion, Iowa Member of K. of P. At Michigan: Member of Webster Society; Illinois Club Court; President of One Year Section. Expects to practice in Iowa. Republican. Permanent address, Ohio, Illinois.

RICHARD APPERSON, Σ X, ... MT. STERLING, KY.

A. B. Centre College, 1891. Attorney-at-law, Kentucky. Born at Mt. Sterling, Kentucky, June 30, 1871. Prepared for college in Centre College Preparatory Department. At Fishburne Academy, Virginia; Medal in prize debating contest; Captain Base Ball Team. Graduated from Centre College, class of '91. Before entering Michigan engaged in banking business. At Michigan, member of '94 Law Base Ball Team. Democrat. Permanent address, Mt. Sterling, Kentucky.

ELMER SYLVESTER AVERY, ... MASON, MICHIGAN.

Attorney-at-law, Michigan, Montana. Took Junior year in 1886–87. Born at Danville, Michigan. In practice 1887–93. Expects to practice in Michigan. Republican. Permanent address, Danville, Michigan.

SEWELL LEE AVERY, Δ T Δ, ... DETROIT, MICH.

Republican.

EARL D. BABST, Ψ Υ, Θ Ν Ε, ... CRESTLINE, OHIO.

Ph. B. Michigan, 1893. One year man. Born at Crestline, Ohio, July 6, 1870, Completed course of Crestline High School, Class of '87. Graduated from Kenyon Military Academy, Class of '89. Entered Kenyon College, Class of '93. At Kenyon: President of Freshman Banquet, [1]; Glee Club, [1], [2]; Leader College Orchestra, [1], [2]; *Collegian* Editor, [2]; Treasurer Athletic Association, [2]; Member of Executive Committee of Ohio State Inter-Collegiate Athletic Association, [2]. Entered Michigan Fall of '91. At Michigan: *Inlander* Editor, [4]; Executive Committee Republican Club, [4]; Toastmaster '93 Foot Ball Banquet, [4]; *Palladium* Editor, [4]; Reception Committee Senior Reception, [4]; Delegate to Sixtieth Annual Convention of Psi Upsilon, [4]. College Editor of *University Magazine* of New York City since 1889. Editor of Western Department of *University Magazine* since August, 1892. College Editor of *College Fraternity* of New York City, 1892–93. Ann Arbor Correspondent of Chicago *Inter Ocean*, 1891–92. Toast '93 Banquet, [5]. Permanent Secretary and Historian, Class of '93 Lit. In Law School: Executive Committee Republican Club; Managing Editor of TO WIT: Republican. Permanent address, Crestline, Ohio.

GEORGE JAFFRAY BUNDAY, Δ T Δ, ... CHICAGO, ILL.

Attended University of Michigan, Class of '93. At Michigan, member of Junior Hop Committee, [2], [3]. Republican. Expects to practice in Chicago, Ill.

GEORGE HOWARD BAILEY, ... MARIETTA, OHIO.

Born at Warren, Washington County, Ohio, February 1, 1867. Before entering Michigan engaged in real estate business at Parkersburg, West Virginia. At Michigan: Member of Webster Society; Ohio Club Court; Cooley Debating Club. Expects to practice in Ohio. Republican. Permanent address, Constitution, Ohio.

EDWARD BURGOYNE BAKER, ... LEAVENWORTH, KANSAS.

Born at Leavenworth, Kansas, 1873. Graduated from Leavenworth High School. Attended Literary Department, University of Michigan, class of '95. Permanent address, Leavenworth, Kansas.

JOSEPH EDMUND BARRELL, ... MIDDLEVILLE, MICH.

Born in Allegan County, Michigan. Before entering Michigan, engaged as assistant civil engineer. Expects to practice in Michigan. Republican. Permanent address, Middleville, Mich.

EUGENE BATAVIA, ... KANSAS CITY, MO.

Born at Breslau, Germany, August 8, 1873. Graduated from Kansas City High School. Attended Literary Department U. of M. Class of '95. In Law School: Manager of Field Sports [1]; Member Board of Directors of U. of M. Athletic Association; Assistant Manager of Varsity Foot Ball Team [2]; To WIT: Editor [2]. Expects to practice in Kansas City, Missouri. Permanent address, 1403 Grand Avenue, Kansas City, Missouri.

ARTHUR D. BATE, ... SAGINAW, MICH.

Born at Saginaw, Michigan, January 1, 1872. Graduated from West Side High School, Class of '92. Graduated from Commercial Department of International Business College of Saginaw. Attended the Literary Department U. of M. 1892–93. Prior to entering Michigan was engaged in mercantile pursuits. At Michigan, member of Mechem Debating Club. Expects to practice in Saginaw, Michigan. Permanent address, Saginaw, Mich.

ALLEN SAMUEL BEACH, ... GARFIELD, WASHINGTON.

Born at Mt. Vernon, Ohio, October 22, 1864. Prepared for college in Belleville, Ohio. Attended Ada Normal School, Ada, Ohio. Before entering Michigan, engaged in teaching. At Michigan: Member of Jeffersonian Society; Columbia River Club Court. Member of Knights of Pythias. Expects to practice at Colfax, Washington. Democrat. Permanent address, Colfax, Washington.

CARL BISMARK BEKEMEYER, ... SPRINGFIELD, ILL.

(No information received).

AARON JOSEPH BESSIE, ... WAHPETON, N. DAKOTA.

Born in New York City, September 23, 1872. Graduated from Wahpeton High School. Before entering Michigan, bank clerk. At Michigan, member of Oregon Moot Court. Expects to practice in New York City. Independent in Politics. Permanent address, Wahpeton, North Dakota.

IRA CHARLES BELDEN, Φ K Ψ, Φ Δ Φ, ... KANEVILLE, ILL.

Ph. B. University of Michigan, 1893. One year man. Born at Kaneville, Illinois, July 2, 1871. Graduated from East Aurora High School, Aurora, Illinois. Entered Michigan Class of '93. At Michigan: '93 Lit Foot Ball Team, [2]; Editor *Yellow and Blue*, [3]; Director Athletic Association, [3]; Editor *Inlander*, [4]; Manager '93 Lit Foot Ball Team, [4]; winner one and two mile bicycle races Field Day, [4]; winner bicycle races Northwestern Inter-Collegiate Field Day at Chicago, June, 1893, [4]; toast '93 Banquet, [5]. Holds University Record for one and two mile bicycle races. Expects to practice at Elgin, Illinois. Democrat. Permanent address, Kaneville, Kane County, Illinois.

CHAUNCEY ROLLA BISHOP, ... HASTINGS, MICH.

One year man. Born in Township of Rutland, Barry County, Michigan. Graduated from Hastings High School, 1891. Teacher in Barry County 1891-92. Law office of William O. Sowden, Hastings, Michigan, 1893. Member of K. O. T. M.; of I. O. G. T. At Michigan, member Michigan Club Court. Republican. Permanent address, Hastings, Michigan.

ALFRED FRANKLIN BISSELL, B Θ Π, Φ Δ Φ, ... ANN ARBOR, MICH.

Attorney-at-law, Michigan. Born at Dexter, Iowa, July 6, 1864. Prepared for college at Western Reserve Academy, Hudson, Ohio, and at Oberlin, Ohio. Attended Adelbert College, class of '93. Before entering Michigan, engaged in teaching. Expects to practice in Iowa. Permanent address, Aurora, Ohio.

MILTON EDWARD BLAKE, Δ X, ... DENVER, COLORADO.

Born at Denver, Colorado, October 14, 1871. Expects to practice at Denver. Republican. Permanent address, Denver, Colorado.

ARTHUR BROWN, ... ANN ARBOR, MICH.

(No information received).

MILO MENOAH BRUCE, ... WINAMAC, IND.

Attorney-at-law, Indiana. Born at Winamac, Indiana, February 10, 1873. Graduated from Lebanon, Ohio, High School, class of '91. Engaged in teaching before entering Michigan. At Michigan, member of Indiana Club Court. Expects to practice at Crown Point, Indiana. Republican. Permanent address, Winamac, Indiana.

DANIEL JOHN BUCKLEY, ... PITTSBURGH, PENN.

Born at Pittsburgh, Pennsylvania, June 4, 1872. Prepared for college in Pittsburgh Central High School. Attended Fordham College, New York City, for three years. At Fordham: Vice-President of Dramatic Association; Treasurer of Athletic Association; First Lieutenant and Adjutant of Battalion. At Michigan: Class Prophet; Invitation Committee Washington Birthday Celebration [2]; member of Jeffersonian Society; Pennsylvania Club Court; Foley Guild. Expects to practice in Pittsburgh, Pennsylvania. Republican. Permanent address, 204 Coltart Square, Oakland, Pittsburgh, Pennsylvania.

MILTON DRAPER BRYCE, ... MARQUETTE, MICH.

Attorney-at-law, Michigan. One year man. Born at Lynn, Michigan, September 30, 1863. Graduated from Romeo, Michigan, High School, Class of '84. Taught school 1884–86. Studied law 1886–88. Admitted to bar at Mt. Clemens, Michigan, 1888. In practice at Marquette, Michigan, 1888–90. Attended Northwestern University 1890–93. Expects to practice at Duluth, Minnesota. Republican (Independent). Permanent address, Ann Arbor, Michigan.

CHARLES ALBERT BULL, ... SUN RIVER, MONT.

Born at Sun River, Montana, February 23, 1874. Attended Terre Haute, Indiana, High School. Republican. Permanent address, Sun River, Montana.

ARCHIBALD FORBES BUNTING, ... FRANKFORT, MICH.

Attorney-at-law. One year man. Born at Albion, Illinois, May 17, 1871. Attended Benzonia College three years At Michigan: Judge Michigan Club Court; President Benton Debating Club; member of Webster Society. Republican. Permanent address, Frankfort, Mich.

CHARLES WILKES BURCH, ... SALINA, KANSAS.

Ph. B., Kansas Wesleyan University, 1891. Born at Williamsport, Indiana, September 5, 1869. Graduated from Salina High School. Graduated from Kansas Wesleyan University, class of '91. At Michigan: Member of Webster Society; Kansas Club Court. Expects to practice in Kansas. Republican. Permanent address, Salina, Kansas.

ALEXANDER GEORGE BURR, ... BOTTINEAU, N. DAKOTA.

Born at Pitrodie, Perthshire, Scotland, February 25, 1871. Engaged in teaching before entering Michigan. At Michigan: Law Vice-President of Prohibition Club [1]; Law Vice-President of Students' Christian Association [2]; member of Webster Society, Benton Debating Club, Kansas Club Court. President of Teachers' Association of Bottineau County for several years. Expects to practice at Grand Forks, North Dakota Prohibitionist. Permanent address, Bottineau, North Dakota.

WILLIAM HENRY BURTNER JR., Σ X, ... HARTWELL, OHIO.

Born at Cincinnati, Ohio. Prepared for college in Hartwell High School. Before entering Michigan, engaged as boat builder. Expects to practice in Cincinnati, Ohio. Permanent address, Cincinnati, Ohio.

HARRY ERNEST CANDLER, Z Ψ, Φ Δ Φ, Θ Φ, ... DETROIT, MICH.

B. S. Michigan, 1892. Attorney-at-law, Michigan. Born at Detroit March 7, 1870. Prepared for college in Detroit High School and Michigan Military Academy. Graduated from University of Michigan Class of '92. At Michigan: Member of Junior Hop Committee, [3]; member of Senior Reception Committee, [4]. Expects to practice in Detroit, Michigan. Republican. Permanent address, 636 Woodward Avenue, Detroit, Michigan.

Charles W. Burdick, Β Θ Π, ... Cheyenne, Wyoming.

Attorney-at-law, Wyoming. One year man. Born at Toledo, Ohio. Prepared for college, Providence, Rhode Island. Attended Ohio Wesleyan University, Delaware, Ohio, class of '81. Expects to practice in Cheyenne, Wyoming. Republican. Permanent address, Cheyenne, Wyoming.

Alvay P. Cady, Φ Α Π, ... Olivet, Mich.

B. S. Olivet College, 1890. Born at Lamont, Michigan, March 29, 1865. Graduated from Olivet College, class of '90. At Olivet: Class President, Senior year; Championship Michigan Inter-Collegiate Athletic Association high-jump [1], [2], [3], [4], record, 5 ft. 4 in. Before entering Michigan, Principal in Public School, Civil Engineer. Expects to practice in Boise City, Idaho. Republican. Permanent address, Hersey, Michigan.

Richard Lee Cameron, ... Marysville, Ohio.

Born at Marysville, Ohio, July 11, 1872. At Michigan, member of Jeffersonian Society. Expects to practice at Marysville, Ohio. Republican. Permanent address, Marysville, Ohio.

Edward Eugene Carr, ... Telluride, Col.

Born at Montezuma, Iowa, August 7, 1868. Before entering Michigan engaged in hotel business. At Michigan: Member Jeffersonian Society; Benton Debating Club. Expects to practice "in the West." Democrat. Permanent address, Neligh, Nebraska.

Rex Ronald Case, Ζ Ψ, Θ Ν Ε, Ω Ν, ... Marquette, Mich.

Born at Lansing, Michigan, August 10, 1874. Prepared for college at Marquette, Michigan. Attended Literary Department U. of M. Class of '95. At Michigan: Toast Freshman Banquet; member of Sophomore Hop Committee; member Junior Hop Committee; Freshman Banjo Club; 'Varsity Banjo Club. Expects to practice at Detroit, Michigan. Republican. Permanent address, Lansing, Michigan.

Charles Whitney Chapman, Δ Χ, ... Detroit, Mich.

Born at Detroit, Michigan, 1872. Prepared for college in Philadelphia. At Michigan: Member of Webster Society; Michigan Club Court. Expects to practice in Detroit. Permanent address, 141 Woodward Avenue, Detroit, Michigan.

Robert Clowry Chapman, Δ Χ, ... Chicago, Ill.

Born at Fort Scott, Kansas, July 28, 1871. Prepared for college in North Division High School, Chicago. Before entering Michigan was for two years in service of Central Union Telephone Company, Chicago. Expects to practice in Chicago. Republican. Permanent address, care of General Solicitor of Central Union Telephone Company, Chicago, Illinois.

Leslie Howard Chatterson, ... Detroit, Mich.

Expects to practice in Chicago, Illlnois. Permanent address, Chicago, Illinois.

Charles Erehart Chadman, ... Conneaut, Ohio.

Prepared for college at Lancaster City High School. Attended Pennsylvania State College, Class of '93. Permanent address, Conneaut, Ohio.

John Franklin Chambers, ... Cheboygan, Mich.

Attorney-at-law, Michigan. One year man. Born at Fair Haven, Michigan, October, 1868. Prepared for college in Cheboygan Public Schools. Student of Albion College. Circuit Court Commissioner, Justice of the Peace, and County Prosecuting Attorney. At Michigan, member of Webster Society. Democrat. Expects to practice "somewhere in the United States." Permanent address, Cheboygan, Michigan.

Frank Edgar Chamberlain, ... Manistee, Mich.

Born at Holland, Sheboygan County, Wisconsin. At Michigan: President Webster Society, [2]; Secretary Webster Society, [1]; Secretary Benton Debating Club; Prosecuting Attorney Michigan Club Court; Vice-President Young Men's Liberal Guild. Member of I. O. G. T. Expects to practice at Manistee. Prohibitionist. Permanent address, 372 Second Street, Manistee, Michigan.

Philip Percy Beaugrand Champagne, Κ Σ, ... Chicago, Ill.

Born at Wausau, Wisconsin, October 19, 1872. Graduated from Merrill, Wisconsin, High School. Attended University of Wisconsin, Class of '92. Before entering Michigan, engaged in lumber business. Member of Knights of Pythias and Masonic orders. Expects to practice in Chicago. Republican. Permanent address, Merrill, Wisconsin.

Ira Albert Clark, ... Clay Center, Ohio.

Born at Clay Center, Ohio, March 22, 1863. Before entering Michigan, Farmer, School Teacher, Justice of the Peace, and Traveling Salesman. Expects to practice in Ohio. Republican. Permanent address, Clay Center, Ohio.

Francis Gilbert Clark, ... Guthrie Centre, Iowa.

(No information received.)

Willis Sherman Clark, ... Marine City, Mich.

(No information received.)

Milton Lee Clawson, ... Greenville, Ohio.

Born at Greenville, Ohio, July 31, 1872. Graduated valedictorian of Class of '92 Greenville Union School, also receiving the McCulloch Scholarship of Adrian College. Before entering Michigan, City Editor of Greenville *Daily Sun*. At Michigan: member of Webster Society, Benton Debating Club, and Oratorical League; Vice-President Prohibition Club, [2]. President of City Club, Greenville. Contributor to newspapers and magazines. Expects to practice at Marion, Indiana, or in Michigan. Prohibitionist. Permanent address, Greenville, Ohio.

HOLBROOK GILSON CLEAVELAND, Ψ Υ, Φ Δ Φ, ... PLYMOUTH, IND.
A. B. Michigan, 1893. Born at Plymouth, Ind., August 13, 1870. Graduated from Smith Academy, St. Louis. Entered Michigan, Class of '93. At Michigan, Tennis Manager, [3]; Director Athletic Association, [3], [4], [5]; Manager 'Varsity Base-Ball Team, [4]; President Northwestern Inter-Collegiate Athletic Association, [4]; Toast '93 Foot-Ball Banquet, [4], [5]; Vice-President Athletic Association, [5]; Member of University Board of Control of Athletics, [5]; Delegate to 24th Convention of Phi Delta Phi, [4]. Expects to practice at St. Louis, Missouri. Democrat. Permanent address, 39 Portland Place, St. Louis, Missouri.

HARVEY KILMER CLOCK, ... ELYRIA, OHIO.
Born at Monroeville, Ohio. Before entering Michigan, publisher of the *Lorain County Reporter*, Elyria, Ohio. Permanent address, Huron, Ohio.

CHARLES EDGAR COCHRAN, ... ALICEL, OREGON.
B. S. D. Oregon Normal School, 1890. Born at Summersville, Oregon, May 8, 1873. Graduated from Union High School, Summersville. Graduated from Oregon Normal School, Class of '90. At Oregon: President of Athletic Association; Treasurer of Class of '90. Before entering Michigan, engaged in teaching, mercantile pursuits, Teller of Farmers' Mortgage and Savings Bank of Summersville. At Michigan, member of Oregon Club Court. Expects to practice at La Grande, Oregon. Democrat. Permanent address, Alicel, Oregon.

CHARLES JOHN COLE, ... COPOPA, OHIO.
A. B. Oberlin, 1886. One year man. Born at Columbia, Ohio, August 19, 1860. Graduated from Oberlin College, Class of '86. At Oberlin: Class Prophet; Editor of *Oberlin Review.* Before entering Michigan: Town Clerk, Justice of Peace, Decennial Appraiser of Real Estate in Columbia, Ohio, school teacher. Expects to practice in Illinois. Republican. Permanent address, Copopa, Ohio.

MATTHEW FRANCIS COLEMAN, ... ALTOONA, PENN.
Born at Hollidaysburg, Pennsylvania, August 3, 1873. Prepared for college in a private school at Altoona. Attended Georgetown College, Washington, District of Columbia. Took Junior year at Georgetown Law School, Washington, District of Columbia. Expects to practice in Pennsylvania. Democrat. Permanent address, 1112, 14th Street, Altoona, Pennsylvania.

VICTOR OTHO COLTRANE, ... CAVE SPRING, MISSOURI.
A. B. Drury College, 1892. Born at Cave Spring, Missouri, December 20, 1868. Prepared for college at Springfield Academy, Springfield, Missouri. Graduated from Drury College, class of '92. At Drury: Second honor in contest of Missouri Inter-Collegiate Oratorical Association, 1892. At Michigan: President of Jeffersonian Society; Valedictorian of Law Class of '94; member of Mechem Debating Club; Missouri Club Court. Expects to practice in Springfield, Missouri. Democrat. Permanent address, Cave Spring, Missouri.

FRED JAMES COCHRAN, ... DETROIT, MICH.

One year man. Born at Parma, Michigan, July 10, 1869. Expects to practice in Detroit. Permanent address, Detroit, Michigan.

OSCAR BRADBURY CONANT, ... WEST DE PERE, WIS.

Born at Appleton, Wisconsin, March 31, 1873. Prepared for College in People's Academy, Morrisville, Vermont. Attended Lawrence University, Appleton, Wisconsin, 1890–92. At Michigan: Member of Webster Literary Society; Benton Debating Club; Treasurer U. of M. Prohibition Club. Expects to practice in Milwaukee. Prohibitionist. Permanent address, West De Pere, Wisconsin.

HERBERT THOMAS CONDON, ... EUGENE, OREGON.

A. B. University of Oregon, 1892. Born at The Dalles, Oregon, St. Patrick's Day, 1870. Graduated from University of Oregon, Class of '92. At Oregon, Class Orator at Commencement Before entering Michigan, engaged in mercantile pursuits. At Michigan, member of Columbia River Club Court. Member of I. O. G. T. Expects to practice "on the Pacific Coast." Republican. Permanent address, Eugene, Oregon.

GRANT CONKLIN, ... SCIPIO, MICH.

Ph. B. Hillsdale, 1892. Born at Scipio, Michigan, June 10, 1865. Graduated from Hillsdale College, class of '92. Before entering Michigan, "Student, Farmer and Teacher." Member of Amphictyon Literary Society at Hillsdale. Expects to practice in Michigan. Democrat. Permanent address, Scipio, Michigan.

NORMAN BRUCE COUNTRYMAN, ... BERKLEY, PENN.

Born in Somerset County, Pennsylvania, May 4, 1869. Prepared for college at Meylesdale Preparatory School. Attended South Western State Normal School of Pennsylvania, class of '90. Before entering Michigan engaged in teaching. At Michigan: Member of Jeffersonian Society; Keystone Club Court. Member of I. O. O. F. Expects to practice in Pennsylvania. Republican. Permanent address, Berkley, Pennsylvania.

THOMAS GRAHAM CROTHERS, Σ N, ... SAN JOSÉ, CAL.

A. B. Leland Stanford Jr. University, 1892. Born at Wapelo, Iowa, November, 1869. Prepared for college in San Jose High School. Graduated from Leland Stanford Jr. University, Class of '92. At Michigan, member of California Club Court. Expects to practice at San Jose, California. Republican. Permanent address, San Jose, California.

JAMES HALLECK CROWELL, ... HALL, PENN.

Ph. B. Trinity College (N. C.), 1892. Born at Goldsboro, Pennsylvania, September 14, 1868. Prepared for college at Phillips Exeter and at New Berlin, Pennsylvania. Graduated from Trinity College (N. C.), class of '92. At Michigan, member of Pennsylvania Club Court. Expects to practice in Pennsylvania. Republican. Permanent address, Hall, Pennsylvania.

Oliver Ellsworth Cramer, ... Rock Island, Ill.
A. B. Augustana College.

Frank Crozier, Σ X, ... Madison, Ind.
B. S. Hanover, 1892. Permanent address, Madison, Indiana.

Alonzo Lonidas Curtis, ... Belton, Texas.
One year man. Born at Bloomfield, Texas, December 5, 1872. Attended University of Texas, 1889–91. Before entering Michigan engaged in teaching. At Michigan, Vice-President Jeffersonian Society. Expects to practice in Texas. Democrat. Permanent address, Moffat, Texas.

Thomas Whitfield Day, ... Rising City, Neb.
Attorney-at-Law, Nebraska. Born at Mt. Clemens, Michigan, November 7, 1865 Attended Rising City High School. Graduated from Mt. Clemens High School. Attended Western Normal and Business College, Iowa, Class of '87. Before entering Michigan engaged in real estate and insurance business. At Michigan, Member of Nebraska Iowa Club Court Member of K. of P., A. O. U. W., M. W. A., Sons of Veterans. Expects to practice in David City, Butler County, Nebraska. Republican. Permanent address, David City, Nebraska.

Charles A. Denison, ... Decatur, Ill.
B. L. Michigan, 1893. Born at Newburg, Illinois, September 24, 1868. Graduated from Decatur High School, Class of '88. Graduated from University of Michigan, Class of '93. At Michigan: Managing Editor *U. of M. Daily*, [4], [5]; President University Press Club, [4]; President Illinois Republican Club, [4]. In Law School: Editor-in-Chief, To Wit: Executive Committee U. of M. Republican Club. Representative of Chicago *Inter Ocean*. Member of F. and A. M. Expects to practice in Decatur, Illinois. Republican. Permanent address, Decatur, Illinois.

Martin John Dillon, ... Galena, Ill.
One year man. Born at Galena, Illinois, March 29, 1873. Attended German-English College. Studied law under E. L. Bedford, Law '68. At Michigan: Member of Illinois Club Court. Expects to practice in Illinois. Democrat. Permanent address, Galena, Illinois.

Charles Orlando Duncan, Δ X, ... Oscoda, Mich.
Attorney-at-Law, Michigan. Born at Brigden, Michigan, July 17, 1865. Before entering college engaged in lumber commission business. Expects to practice in Oscoda, Michigan. Republican. Permanent address, Oscoda, Michigan.

Frank Harry Dunnahoo, ... South Bend, Ind.
One year man Born at South Bend, Indiana, April 5, 1873. Before entering Michigan, school teacher and law student. At Michigan, Member of Indiana Club Court Expects to practice in South Bend, Indiana. Democrat. Permanent address, South Bend, Indiana.

Ulysses Grant Denman, ... Wilshire, Ohio.

Born at Wilshire, Ohio, November 24, 1866. Prepared for college in public schools of Wilshire. Attended National Normal University, Lebanon, Ohio; Northern Indiana Normal School, Valparaiso, Indiana. Before entering Michigan, Superintendent of schools for three years at Wilshire. At Michigan: Member of Webster Society Expects to practice in Ohio. Republican. Permanent address, Wilshire, Ohio.

Irving William Durfee, Δ Υ, ... Detroit, Mich.

Born at Plymouth, Michigan, November 20, 1868. Prepared for college in Plymouth and Ann Arbor High Schools. Attended University of Michigan two years with Class of '92, one year with Class of '93, At Michigan, Editor of '93 *Palladium*. Expects to practice in Detroit, Michigan. Permanent address, Δ Υ House, Ann Arbor, Michigan.

Lucian Johnson Eastin, ... Kearney, Mo.

One year man. Born at Kearney, Missouri, July 12, 1868. Attended State Normal School, Warrensburg, Missouri. Before entering Michigan engaged in teaching. In law office of Hon. D. C. Allen, Liberty, Missouri, 1892–93. At Michigan, Member of Jeffersonian Society and Missouri Club Court. Expects to practice in Missouri. Democrat. Permanent address, Kearney, Clay County, Missouri.

Emma Eaton, ... Iowa.

One year student. Born at Black River Falls, Wisconsin, 1868. Before entering Michigan engaged as Examiner of Titles. Teacher in public schools of Minneapolis. Attended Wisconsin State Normal School. At Michigan: Secretary Law Class of '94, Clerk of Practice Court, member of Webster Society, Nebraska-Iowa Club Court. Expects to practice in Creston, Iowa. Prohibitionist. Permanent address, Creston, Iowa.

Walter Abijah Eckles, ... Marshalltown, Iowa.

B. C. E., Cornell College, Iowa, 1892 One year man. Born in Marshall County, Iowa, March 18, 1869. Prepared for college at Albion Seminary, Albion, Iowa. Graduated from Cornell College, Class of '92. At Cornell: Valedictorian of Literary Society; Right Tackle, Foot-Ball Team; winner of mile run, time 5 min. 3½ sec.; winner of 440-yard dash, time 52½ sec. At Michigan: Honorable mention in Mechem prize, member Webster Society, Iowa-Nebraska Club Court. Expects to practice in Iowa. Republican. Permanent address, Marshalltown, Iowa.

Daniel Abraham Edwards, ... Cadillac, Mich.

Born in Huron County, Michigan, September 16, 1866. Before entering Michigan engaged in teaching. In 1889 was Democratic candidate for legislature, being defeated by a plurality of 36 votes. At Michigan: Member of Webster Society, Michigan Club Court. Expects to practice in Grand Rapids. Democrat. Permanent address, Cadillac, Mich.

WILLIS VICTOR ELLIOTT, Δ X, ... DENVER, COLO.

Born at Mansfield, Pennsylvania, June 13, 1871. Prepared for college in Denver High School and Pennsylvania State Normal School. Expects to practice in Denver, Colorado. Republican. Permanent address, Denver, Colorado.

JOHN ALBERT ELLIS, ... ANN ARBOR, MICH.

(No information received.)

HENRI FRANK ESHLEMAN, ... MARTICKVILLE, LANE CO., PA.

B. E., 1890; M. E., 1892, Pennsylvania State Normal School. One year man. Born at MarticKville, Pennsylvania, August 28, 1869. Graduated from Pennsylvania State Normal School, Class of '90. Principal of Training Department of Pennsylvania State Normal School, and Lecturer in Pedagogics in same institution 1891-93. Expects to practice in Lancaster, Pennsylvania. Republican. Permanent address, Lancaster, Pennsylvania.

GEORGE MARK EVANS, ... FORT GRATIOT, MICH.

(No information received.)

HARVEY ARETAS EVANS, ... METROPOLIS, ILL.

B. S., Southern Normal College, 1888; A. B., 1889. Born in Massac County, Illinois, August 1, 1854. Graduated from Southern Normal College, Class of '88. Before entering Michigan engaged in teaching. At Michigan: Member of Illinois Club Court. Member of I. O. O. F. Expects to practice in Illinois. "Democrat *in sempiternum*." Permanent address, Metropolis, Illinois.

GEORGE DUDLEY FAIRBANKS, ... DENISON, TEXAS.

Born at Sedalia, Missouri, November 4, 1872. Attended the Ball High School, Galveston, Texas. Before entering Michigan, engaged on a surveying corps, in an insurance office, bookkeeper in a bank. At Michigan, member of Jeffersonian Society. Expects to practice in Texas Republican. Permanent address, Denison, Texas.

GEORGE FRANKLIN FELTS, ... FORT WAYNE, IND.

Born at College Corner, Indiana. Prepared for college in Preparatory Department of Purdue University. Attended Michigan State Normal School, Class of '83. Member of Irving Society at Purdue, Olympic Society at Michigan Normal. Before entering Michigan, County Superintendent of Public Schools, Ft. Wayne, Indiana. Member of Masonic orders. Democrat. Permanent address, Ft. Wayne, Indiana.

RAYMOND MARSHALL FERGUSON, ... MIDDLEVILLE, MICH.

Born at Chicago, July 14, 1871. Prepared for college in Ann Arbor High School. Attended the Literary Department of U. of M., Class of '93. In Law School, member of Michigan Club Court. Expects to practice in Grand Rapids, Michigan. Republican. Permanent address, Middleville, Michigan.

LEONARD FISKE, ... CONCORD, MASS.

Born at Bethel, Vermont, February 8, 1869. Graduated from Randolph Normal School, Class of '85. Graduated from Concord High School, Class of '90. At University of Vermont, 1890-91. In law office of Hon. D. J. Foster, Burlington, Vermont, 1891-92. At Michigan: Chairman Executive Committee of Democratic Club; member of Webster Society. Democrat. Permanent address, Concord, Massachusetts.

CHARLES FITZGERALD, ... KENTLAND, IND.

Born at Kentland, Indiana, April 14, 1872 Engaged in school teaching before entering Michigan. Democrat. Permanent address, Kentland, Indiana.

LUTHER BLANCHARD FREEMAN, ... ST. PAUL, MINN.

Born at Fort Shaw, Montana, November 27, 1870. Prepared for college at Kenyon Military Academy, Class of '89. Attended Ohio Wesleyan University. At O. W. U., member of 'Varsity Base-Ball Team. Before entering Michigan, in law office, Delaware, Ohio. Expects to practice in the "Great West." Republican. Permanent address, St. Paul, Minnesota.

BENJAMIN FRANKLIN FRIEND, ... CRESTON, IOWA.

Born in New York City, August 11, 1874. Graduated from Creston High School, Class of '92. At Michigan, member of Iowa-Nebraska Club Court. Expects to practice in New York State. Republican. Permanent address, Creston, Iowa.

GEORGE WASHINGTON FULLER, Κ Σ, ... POTSDAM, N. Y.

Born at Potsdam, New York, February 22, 1868. Graduated from Potsdam State Normal and Training School, Class of '89. Before entering Michigan, principal of public schools in New York State. At Michigan: President, Vice-President and member of Executive Committee U. of M. Republican Club; member of Washington's Birthday Committee; delegate to National Republican College League, Syracuse, New York, [2]; Editor of TO WIT: Member of Masonic orders. Expects to practice in New York City. Republican. Permanent address, Potsdam, N. Y.

WALTER SHEPPARD FULTON, Φ Δ Φ, ... SEATTLE, WASHINGTON.

One year man. Born at Pittsburgh, Pennsylvania, August 10, 1873. Prepared for college in Seattle High School. Attended University of Washington. Expects to practice in Seattle, Washington. Democrat. Permanent address, Seattle, Washington.

CLIFTON DE WITT GORDON, ... YPSILANTI, MICH.

Born at Bell Branch, Michigan, October 14, 1869. Son of Capt. George C. Gordon, law '61. Attended Michigan State Normal School, 1887-88, 1889-91. Principal of Steven's School, Highland Park, Michigan, 1891-92. At Michigan, member of Webster Society. Member of Detroit Tent, No. 570, K. O. T. M. Expects to practice in Detroit. Republican. Permanent address, Detroit, Mich.

WILLIAM J. GALBRAITH, ... GARDNER, ILL.

Born at Atwater, Illinois, November 5, 1866. Attended Illinois State Normal School, and Literary Department University of Michigan. In Law School, member of Webster Society, Illinois Club Court. Expects to practice in "United States." Republican.

GEORGE JACOB GENEBACH, ... BROOKLYN, MICH.

Born at Brooklyn, Michigan, June 29, 1874. Attended Brooklyn High School and Michigan State Normal School. Graduated from Cleary Business College, Ypsilanti, Michigan, class of '92. At Michigan: Treasurer of Jeffersonian Society; member Michigan Club Court, Oratorical Association. Expects to practice in Detroit. Democrat. Permanent address, Brooklyn, Michigan.

CYRUS WILLIAM GEORGE, Δ Τ Δ, ... ENGLEWOOD, ILL.

Born at Englewood, Illinois. Prepared for college at Michigan Military Academy. Expects to practice at Lake Charles, Louisiana. Democrat. Permanent address, 356 Chestnut Street, Englewood, Illinois.

VLADIMIR AUGUST GERINGER, ... CHICAGO, ILL.

Ph. B. Michigan, 1893. Born at Chicago, October 25, 1872. Prepared for college in Chicago West Division High School. Graduated from University of Michigan, Class of '93. Expects to practice in Chicago. Permanent address, 150 West 12th Street, Chicago, Illinois.

GEORGE GERLACH, ... ANN ARBOR, MICH.

Born at Northfield, Washtenaw County, Michigan, "A. D. 1863." Before entering Michigan, farmer and mechanic, Township Clerk 1892–92, School Moderator 1889–92, member of County Democratic Committee. Democrat. Permanent address, Box 1121, Ann Arbor, Michigan.

GEORGE JOHN GLEIM, ... OTTAWA, ILL.

Born at Ottawa, Illinois, April 6, 1872. Prepared for college in Ottawa High School. At Michigan, member of Jeffersonian Society. Expects to practice either in Ottawa or Chicago. Democrat, "straight out and faithful." Permanent address, 658 North Main Street, Ottawa, Illinois.

EVAN BENSON GOSS, ... ROCKFORD, MICH.

Born at Rockford, Michigan, December 8, 1872. Prepared for college in Rockford High School. At Michigan, member of Webster Society. Before entering Michigan, was engaged in teaching Expects to practice in Grand Rapids. Prohibitionist. Permanent address, Rockford, Michigan.

DANIEL HENRY GRADY, ... COLUMBUS, WIS.

One year man. Born at Columbus, Wisconsin, August 13, 1872. In law office of John S. Maxwell. 1891–93. At Michigan, member of Jeffersonian Society. Expects to practice in Milwaukee. Democrat. Permanent address, Columbus, Wisconsin.

HUMPHREY SNELL GRAY, ... LUDINGTON, MICH.

A. B. Michigan, 1893. Born in Canada, September 8, 1868. Before entering Michigan, lumber inspector. Graduated from U. of M., Class of '93. In Law School: member of Clio Club, Michigan Club Court. Candidate for A. M. degree at U. of M. Expects to practice in Michigan. Republican. Permanent address, Londesborough, Ontario, Canada.

GEORGE HALVERSON, ... OGDEN, UTAH.

Born at Ogden, Utah, November 25, 1868. Graduated in Normal course from University of Utah, class of '88. At Utah, Valedictorian, class of '88. Before entering Michigan was engaged in teaching. At Michigan, member of Cooley Debating Club. Expects to practice in Ogden, Utah. Republican. Permanent address, Ogden, Utah.

LOUIS HEATON HANNA, ... MONMOUTH, ILL.

(No information received).

JAMES JOSEPH HARRINGTON, ... O'NEILL, NEB

Born at Lindsay, Ontario, October 29, 1869. Attended Lindsay Separate School. Graduated from Omaha Commercial College, Omaha, Nebraska, class of '89. Before entering Michigan in real estate and insurance business. At Michigan: Member Webster Society; Griffin Debating Club; Iowa-Nebraska Club Court. Expects to practice in Sioux City, Iowa. Democrat. Permanent address, O'Neill, Nebraska.

HYRUM SMITH HARRIS, ... MONROE, UTAH.

Born at Smithfield, Utah, October 2, 1860. Graduated from Brigham Young Academy, class of '85. Before entering Michigan engaged in teaching. At Michigan; Member of Utah Debating Society, Utah Club Court. Expects to practice in Richfield, Utah. Democrat. Permanent address, Monroe, Sevier County, Utah.

WALTER CUNNINGHAM HARTMAN, ... AUBURN, IND.

Born at South Bend, Indiana, February 11, 1873. Prepared for college in Auburn Commissioned High School. Before entering Michigan, Notary Public, in insurance business. At Michigan: President of Jeffersonian Society; Judge U. of M. Supreme Court; member of Indiana Club Court. Expects to practice in Auburn, Indiana. Republican. Permanent address, Auburn, Indiana.

DENNIS B. HAYES, ... ADRIAN, MICH

Born at Adrian, Michigan, November 11, 1867. Graduated from Adrian High School, class of '89. Attended Adrian College three years. Before entering Michigan in mercantile pursuits. Took Junior year of law at Georgetown Law School, Washington, District of Columbia. At Georgetown, Treasurer of '94 Law class. At Michigan, Member of Foley Guild. Expects to practice in Detroit, Michigan. Democrat. Permanent address, 13 N. Main St., Adrian, Michigan.

NATHAN JOHN HARRIS, ... HARRISVILLE, UTAH.

Born at Harrisville, Utah. Attended University of Deseret, Salt Lake City, 1884-86. At Michigan, member of Utah Literary and Debating Society. Expects to practice in Ogden, Utah. Republican. Permanent address, Harrisville, Utah.

JOSEPH ALMA HARRIS, ... MONROE, UTAH.

Born at Virgin City, Utah. Before entering Michigan engaged in ranch farming and mining. At Michigan, Member of Utah Debating Club. Secretary Democratic League of Monroe. Expects to practice in Utah. Democrat. Permanent address, Monroe, Utah.

WILLIAM MORRIS HARRISON, ... IPE, TENN.

B. S. Maryville College, 1891. One year man. Born at Ipe, Tennessee, December 9, 1869. Professor in Tulograhler College, 1891-93. Graduated from Maryville High School. Graduated from Maryville College, class of '91. At Maryville, Salutatorian of the class of '91. At Michigan, member of Webster Society and Cooley Debating Club. Member of F. and A. M. Expects to practice in Chattanooga, Tennessee. Republican. Permanent address, Ipe, Tennessee.

RALPH WHITE HARTZELL, Δ T Δ, ... CANTON, OHIO.

Expects to practice in Denver, Colorado. Permanent address, Denver, Colorado.

JAMES MARK HARVEY, JR., ... CONSTANTINE, MICH.

Member of Webster Society. Republican.

WILLIAM PERRY HARVEY, ... BANGOR, MICH.

Born at Bangor, Michigan, January 1, 1870. Prepared for college in Bangor High School. Engaged in teaching prior to entering Law Department. At Michigan: Member Webster Society; Mechem Debating Club; Michigan Club Court; Director Students Lecture Association. Expects to practice at Grand Rapids, Michigan. Republican. Permanent address, Bangor, Michigan.

JOHN HARVEY HASSINGER, ... SHEFFIELD, PENN.

Born at Centreville, Pennsylvania, August 6, 1869. Attended Pennsylvania State Normal School At Michigan: Member of Webster Society; Pennsylvania Club Court. Member of Masonic orders. Expects to practice in Pennsylvania. Independent in politics. Permanent address, Sheffield, Pennsylvania.

FRED HOSEA HATHHORN, ... LIVINGSTON, MONT.

Born in Meagher County, Montana, August 12, 1873. Engaged in teaching before entering Michigan. At Michigan: Member of Webster Society; Mechem Debating Club; Pacific Coast Court. Expects to practice in Montana. Republican. Permanent address, Livingston, Montana.

JOHN MCALLASTER HADDOCK, Φ Δ Θ, ... BEDFORD, IOWA.

Born at Russellville, Arkansas, March 27, 1872. Attended University of Iowa, Class of '94. Permanent address, Bedford, Iowa.

ROBERT CHARLES HENDERSON, ... NORWAY, MICH.

Born at Altoona, Pennsylvania, 1871. Prepared for college in public schools. Before entering Michigan, telegraph operator. Studied law at Norway, Michigan. Expects to practice at Norway, Michigan. Democrat. Permanent address, Norway, Michigan.

EDWIN CHARLES CLEVELAND HENNING, Σ Χ, . . . CANNELTON, IND.

Born at Cannelton, Indiana, January 20, 1875. Graduated from Cannelton High School. Attended University of the South, and De Pauw University, class of '93. At Michigan, member of Indiana Club Court. Expects to practice at New Albany, Indiana. Republican. Permanent address, Cannelton, Indiana.

LOTT RUSSELL HERRICK, Σ Χ, ... FARMER CITY, ILL.

B. L. University of Illinois, 1892. Born at Farmer City, Illinois, December 8, 1871. Graduated from Farmer City High School. At University of Illinois, Vice-President of class of '92. At Michigan: Historian Law Class of '94; Associate-Justice Illinois Club Court. Expects to practice in Farmer City, Illinois Democrat. Permanent address, Farmer City, Illinois.

WILLIAM RHODES HERVEY, K. A. (*Southern Order*), Φ Δ Φ, SANTA ANA, CAL.

B. S. Arkansas State University, 1890. Born at Somerville, Tennessee, March 26, 1870. Graduated from Arkansas State University, class of '90. Democrat. Permanent address, Santa Ana, California.

ALBERT SYLVESTER HINDS, ... MUSKEGON, MICH.

Attorney-at-Law, Michigan. One year man. Born at Muskegon, October 30, 1871. Graduated from Muskegon High School, class of '90. Before entering Michigan, school teacher. At Michigan, member of Michigan Club Court. Expects to practice in Michigan. Republican. Permanent address, 139 Monroe Ave., Muskegon, Michigan.

JOHN LAWRENCE HOLLANDER, ... KALAMAZOO, MICH.

Attorney-at-Law, Michigan. One year man. Born at Kalamazoo, 1872. At Michigan, member of Michigan Club Court. Republican. Permanent address, Kalamazoo, Michigan.

WARREN WILLIAM HOLLIDAY, Σ Χ, ... INDIANAPOLIS, IND.

Born at Indianapolis, June 16, 1872. Graduated from Ohio Military Institute, class of '92. At O. M. I., Secretary Athletic Association; Captain Foot-Ball Team two years; Member Base-Ball Team two years; Senior Captain of Batallion. At Michigan: Member '94 Law Foot-Ball Team; '94 Law Base Ball Team; 2nd prize Middle Weight Boxing, Indoor Meet, March, 1893. Expects to practice in Indianapolis. Democrat. Permanent address, Indianapolis, Indiana.

Bernard Joseph Hope, ... Lovelton, Penn.

B. E., M. E., Pennsylvania State Normal School. One year man. Born at Lovelton, Pennsylvania, November 11, 1866. Prepared for college in Susquehanna Collegiate Institute. Graduated from Pennsylvania State Normal School, Class of '91. Before entering Michigan engaged in teaching. At Michigan, Member of Keystone Club Court, Foley Guild. Expects to practice in Wilkes Barre, Pennsylvania. Democrat. Permanent address, Lovelton, Pennsylvania.

Orestes Easten Hopkins, ... Lyons, Kan.

Born at Williamsport, Indiana, November 29, 1868. Graduated from Salina, Kansas High School. Attended Kansas Wesleyan University, Class of '92. At Kansas: Secretary Kansas State Oratorical Association 1890-91. At Michigan: Member of Kansas Club Court. Expects to practice in Kansas. Republican. Permanent address, Lyons, Kansas.

Sherman Henry Hoverter, ... Reading, Penn.

Born at Lebanon, Pennsylvania, December 24, 1866. Prepared for college in Philadelphia. Attended Lebanon Valley College, Class of '82. Before entering Michigan engaged as professional accountant. At Michigan: Member of Jeffersonian Society; Keystone Club Court. Member of Patriotic Order Sons of America. Expects to practice in Reading, Pennsylvania. Republican. Permanent address, 28 North 11th St., Reading, Pennsylvania.

William Jeremiah Howard, ... Howell, Mich.

Born at White Oak, Ingham County, Michigan, July 16, 1871. Prepared for college in High Schools of Fowlerville and Ann Arbor, Michigan. Attended Michigan Agricultural College, Class of '94. Engaged in teaching before entering Michigan. At Michigan: Member of Jeffersonian Society; Michigan Club Court; Griffin Debating Club. Democrat. Permanent address, Iosca, Michigan.

Harland Bradley Howe, ... Lyndonville, Ver.

Born at Saint Johnsburg, Vermont, February 19, 1873. Entered Michigan with Class of '93, but at the end of his Junior year accepted a position in the office of Hon. Henry C. Ide, of Saint Johnsburg, who in September, 1893, was appointed Chief Justice of Samoa. Democrat. Permanent address, Lyndonville, Vermont.

Charles Adam James, ... Ursa, Ill.

Attorney-at Law, Missouri. Born at Mendon, Illinois, January 12, 1870. Graduated from Gem City Business College, Quincy, Illinois, 1891. In law office, 1891-92. At Michigan: Member of Webster Society, Griffin Debating Club, Illinois Club Court, S. C. A. Member of F. and A. M., and R. A. M. Expects to practice in Quincy, Illinois. Prohibitionist. Permanent address, Ursa, Adams County, Illinois.

J. STANLEY HURD, Ψ Υ, Φ Δ Φ, ... DETROIT, MICH.

A. B. University of Michigan, 1893. Born at Detroit, Michigan, June, 1872. Graduated from Detroit High School, class of '89. Graduated from University of Michigan, class of '93. Expects to practice in Detroit. Republican. Permanent address, Detroit, Michigan.

JOHN JERAULD INGLE, Σ X, ... SAN DIEGO, CAL.

One year man. Born at Evansville, Indiana, 1873. Prepared for college at Woodstock, Illinois, and Beloit College Academy. Attended Beloit College, Class of '94. Expects to practice in Los Angeles, California. Permanent address, San Diego, Cal.

SAMUEL PASHLEY IRWIN, ... ANN ARBOR, MICH.

One year man. Born at Lodi, Wisconsin, February 19, 1870. Has had High School preparation. Before entering Michigan, telegraph operator. Republican. Permanent address, Lodi, Wis.

GEORGE HENRY KANE, ... ALLEGHANY CITY, PENN.

A. B., Duquesne College, 1892. One year man. Born at Alleghany City, September 21, 1870. Prepared for college in Curry Institute, Pittsburg, Pennsylvania. Graduated from Duquesne College, Class of '92. At Duquesne: President of class; Member of Prometheam Literary Society. Expects to practice in Pittsburg, Pennsylvania. Democrat. Permanent address, Perrysville Avenue, Alleghany, Pennsylvania.

WILLIAM CHRISTOPHER KENAGA, ... KANKAKEE, ILL.

Born on Black Friday, Kankakee. Graduated from Kankakee High School. Attended University of Illinois 1889–91. At Illinois: Secretary and Treasurer Illinois Inter-Collegiate Athletic Association 1890-91; Business Manager '93's *Sophograph*. Before entering Michigan engaged in mercantile pursuits, Deputy County Clerk, City Editor *Kankakee Daily Times*. At Michigan, member of Illinois Club Court. Expects to practice in Illinois. Republican. Permanent address, Kankakee, Illinois.

FRED ALONZO KIES, ... JONESVILLE, MICH.

Born at Moscow, Michigan, August 11, 1868. Graduated from Concord, Michigan, High School, Class of '88. Attended Cleary Business College, Ypsilanti, Michigan. At Michigan, member of Michigan Club Court. Member of F. and A. M., R. A. M., R. and S. M., and Knights of Pythias. Expects to practice in Michigan. Democrat. Permanent address, Jonesville, Michigan.

SAMUEL DENTON KINNE, Σ Φ, ... ANN ARBOR, MICH.

Attorney-at-Law, Michigan. Born at Ann Arbor, July 13, 1869. Prepared for college in Ann Arbor High School, Class of '88. Attended Literary Department U. of M. 1889–92. At Michigan: Member Sophomore Hop Committee, [2]; Member Junior Hop Committee, [3]. Expects to practice "somewhere in United States." Independent in politics. Permanent address, Ann Arbor, Michigan.

TORAZO KIKUCHI, ... TOKIO, JAPAN.

Born at Aketaken, Japan, July 11, 1869. At Michigan: Member of the Imperial Historical Society; Eastern Asia Literary Society; Ancient Japanese and Chinese Literary Society. Permanent address, Ann Arbor, Mich.

JOHN JAMES KILEY, ... SCOFIELD, MICH.

Born at Scofield, Michigan, December 9, 1871. Attended Michigan State Normal School, Class of '91. At Michigan, member of Michigan Club Court. Democrat. Permanent address, Scofield, Michigan.

JOSEPH EDGAR KIRBY, ... TEXARKANA, ARK.

A. B., Searcy College, 1891. Born at Texarkana, Arkansas, June 25, 1872. Graduated from Searcy College, Class of '91. At Searcy: Class President; Editor *Searcy Collegian*. Expects to practice in San Antonio, Texas. Democrat. Permanent address, Texarkana, Texas.

WALTER HERMANN KIRK, Φ Κ Ψ, ... PEORIA, ILL.

Born in Kansas, December 5, 1870. Graduated from Peoria High School. Attended University of Michigan, Class of '90. Before entering Michigan, engaged as accountant in life insurance business. Notary Public. At Michigan, contributor to *Inlander*. Expects to practice in Illinois. Republican. Permanent address, Peoria, Illinois.

JACOB KOENIGSTEIN, ... NORFOLK, NEB.

Born at Belleville, Illinois, 1870. Prepared for college at Watertown, Wisconsin. Attended Northwestern University. At Northwestern, Catcher of 'Varsity Base-Ball Team. At Michigan: Member of Nebraska-Iowa Club Court; Catcher of '94 Law Base-Ball Team. Before entering Michigan, cashier of a bank on Santee Indian Reservation. Expects to practice in Nebraska. Democrat. Permanent address, Norfolk, Nebraska.

JOHN KROODSMA, ... GRAND RAPIDS, MICH.

(No information received.)

FRANZ CHRISTIAN KUHN, Φ Δ Φ, ... MT. CLEMENS, MICH.

B. S. Michigan, 1893. Born at Detroit, Michigan, February 8, 1872. Graduated from Mt. Clemens High School. Graduated from University of Michigan, Class of '93. At Michigan: Freshman Banquet Committee, [1]; Invitation Committee, Republican Club Banquet, [3]; Delegate of U. of M. Republican Club to National Convention of Republican League, held at Buffalo, N. Y., [3]; Chairman Arrangements Committee, Senior Reception, [4]; Business Manager of *Castalian*, [4]; Toast '93 Banquet, [5]. In Law School: Member of Michigan Club Court; Assistant Business Manager To WIT: Delegate to National Republican College League, Syracuse, N. Y., 1894. Member of K. of P. Republican. Permanent address, Mt. Clemens, Michigan.

CHARLES HENRY KUBAT, ... CEDAR RAPIDS, IOWA.

Born at Cedar Rapids, Iowa, July, 1871. Prepared for college in Cedar Rapids High School. Before entering Michigan, engaged as clothing salesman. At Michigan, Member of Iowa-Nebraska Moot Court. Member of Knights of Pythias. Expects to practice in Iowa. Democrat. Permanent address, Cedar Rapids, Iowa.

WILLIAM JOHN LANDMAN, ... GRAND RAPIDS, MICH.

Born at Boston, Massachusetts, July 23, 1873. Graduated from Grand Rapids High School, Class of '92. At Michigan: President of Webster Society; Member of Cooley Debating Club; Michigan Club Court. Expects to practice at Grand Rapids. Republican. Permanent address, Grand Rapids, Michigan.

OSCAR JAY LARSON, Α Τ Ω, ... CALUMET, MICH.

B. S., Valparaiso, 1891. Born at Uleaborg, Finland. Came to America in 1874. Graduated from Calumet High School. Graduated from Indiana Normal School, Class of '91. Special student Literary Department, U. of M., 1891-92. In Law School: Member of Webster Society; Michigan Club Court; Base-Ball Manager of '94 Law Team. Has held clerkship in Auditor-General's office, Lansing, Michigan. Expects to practice in Calumet, Michigan. Republican. Permanent address, Calumet, Michigan.

JOHN ADOLPH LENTZ, ... ANN ARBOR, MICH.

Born at Ann Arbor, Michigan, April 20, 1874. Graduated from Ann Arbor High School, Class of '92. Will probably practice in Michigan. Democrat. Permanent address, 22 East Washington Street, Ann Arbor, Michigan.

EDWARD FLEURY LEGENDRE, ... LUDINGTON, MICH.

Attorney-at-Law, Michigan. Born at Ludington, February 19, 1867. Prepared for college in Public Schools of Ludington. Before entering Michigan engaged in teaching; Reporter on *Ludington Daily Mail;* Justice of the Peace. At Michigan: Member of Webster Society; Michigan Club Court. Expects to practice in Ludington. Democrat. Permanent address, Ludington, Michigan.

GEORGE EDWARD LEONARD, ... CEDAR RAPIDS, IOWA.

B. S., Coe College, 1892. Born at Cedar Rapids, Iowa, April 30, 1871. Graduated from Cedar Rapids High School. At Coe College: President of Literary Society; President of Athletic Association; President and Vice-President of Oratorical Association. At Michigan: Member of Jeffersonian Society; Iowa-Nebraska Court; Member of Washington Birthday Committee, [1], [2], Delegate to National Republican College League, Syracuse, N. Y., [2]. Expects to practice in Iowa. Republican. Permanent address, Cedar Rapids, Iowa.

EDWARD BARTHOLOMEW LINEHAN, ... DUBUQUE, IOWA.

(No information received).

ARTHUR MAURICE LEWALD, Ψ Υ, Σ Ξ, ... BURLINGTON, IOWA.

A. B. Union, 1892. One year man. Born at Port Henry, New York, August 21, 1871. Graduated from Elmira Free Academy, Elmira, New York, Valedictorian, Class of '89. Graduated from Union College, Class of '92. At Union: Sigma Xi Scholarship Key; Member of Adelphic Literary Society; Shakespeare Club; Western Club; 'Varsity Banjo Club. Before entering Michigan in law office, 1892–93. At Michigan: Honorable mention Mechem Prize; Member of Benton Debating Club; Iowa-Nebraska Club Court. Expects to practice in Burlington, Iowa. Democrat. Permanent address, Burlington, Iowa.

HARRY PRATT LEWIS, ... BATTLE CREEK, MICH.

Born at Battle Creek, Michigan, October 15, 1870. Graduated from Battle Creek High School, Class of '90. Expects to practice in Battle Creek. Democrat. Permanent address, 103 Fountain Street, Battle Creek, Michigan.

JOHN H. LEWMAN, ... DANVILLE, ILL.

Born at Danville, Illinois, December 28, 1869. Graduated from Danville High School. Attended Cornell University two years. Before entering Michigan in a law office at Danville for one year. At Michigan: Member of Webster Society; Griffin Debating Club; Illinois Club Court. Expects to practice in Danville, Illinois. Democrat. Permanent address, Danville, Illinois.

LEWIS BONNER LINDSAY, Σ Α Ε, ... GAINESVILLE, TEXAS.

Born at Gainesville, Texas, August 31, 1872. Attended University of Texas, Class of '93. At Texas, Base-Ball Manager, 1892. At Michigan: '94 *Palladium* Editor; Member of Southern Moot Court; Executive Committee, U. of M. Democratic Club. Democrat. Permanent address, Gainesville, Texas.

HARRY CLAY LIVENGOOD, ... CAMERON, MISSOURI.

Born at Sharpsburgh, Alleghany County, Pennsylvania. Attended Cameron Public Schools. Graduated from Mrs. Tiernan's Academy, Class of '92. At Michigan: Member of Jeffersonian Society; Missouri Club Court. Expects to practice at Cameron, Missouri. Republican. Permanent address, Cameron, Missouri.

IRA MILTON LONG, ... NILES, MICH.

Born at Niles, Michigan, April 30, 1865. Prepared for college in Ann Arbor High School. Graduated in Art Department and Teacher's Course from Indiana State Normal School. Attended Literary Department U. of M. three years in Ph. B. Course, Class of '89. Before entering Law School, portrait artist, teacher. In real estate business in Washington and Oregon 1889–92. Member of F. & A. M. Expects to practice in Washington or Oregon. Republican. Permanent address, Buchanan, Michigan.

JESSE B. LUSE, ... CARMICHAELS, PENN.

(No information received.)

WILLIAM BRYAN LOCKE, ... OLMSTED FALLS, OHIO.

Born at Brunswick, Ohio, May 21, 1872. Prepared for college in Olmsted Falls High School. Attended Baldwin University, Berea, Ohio, Class of '92. Before entering Michigan engaged in teaching. At Michigan, member of Ohio Club Court. Expects to practice in New York City. Democrat. Permanent address, Olmsted Falls, Ohio.

CHARLES PARKER LOCKE, ... LANSING, MICH.

B. S. Agricultural College, 1891. One year man. Born in Township of Eaton, Ionia County, Michigan. Graduated from Belding High School. Graduated from Michigan Agricultural College, Class of '91. At M. A. C., Vice-President Student's Organization. Before entering Michigan clerk in Attorney-General's office, 1892–93. Expects to practice in Detroit, Michigan. Democrat. Permanent address, Belding, Michigan.

ELIAS WESLEY MARLATT, ... BEAVER FALLS, PENN.

A. B. Geneva College, 1892. Born in Allegheny County, Pennsylvania, October 16, 1869. Graduated from Geneva College, Class of '92. At Geneva: Editor of *College Journal*, [1], [2], [3]; Editor-in-chief of same, [4]; Prize Essay in Rhetoric; Prize Oration. At Michigan: Member of Jeffersonian Society; Keystone Club Court. Expects to practice in Indiana. Republican. Permanent address, Beaver Falls, Pennsylvania.

FREDERICK WILLIAM MARSH, Β Θ Π, ... MT. PLEASANT, IOWA.

One year man. Born at Burlington, Iowa, September 10, 1872. Prepared for college at Fort Mead, Florida. Attended Florida State College and Iowa Wesleyan. Class of '92. At Florida; Medal for best scholarship, 1889–90. At Wesleyan; Major of Batallion. Expects to practice "either in the South or West." Republican. Permanent address, Mt. Pleasant, Iowa.

DAVID JAMES MARSHALL, ... IMLAY CITY, MICH.

Born at Imlay City, January 8, 1871. Graduated from Ann Arbor High School, Class of '92. Republican Permanent address, Imlay City, Michigan.

DARWIN THOMAS MASON, Σ N, ... DEADWOOD, S. DAK.

B. A. Cornell College, 1891. One year man. Graduated from Cornell College, Class of '91. At Cornell: Class President; President of Adelphian Literary Society; President of Athletic Association; Ranking Officer in College Battalion. Before entering Michigan, Private Secretary of Assistant Superintendent of C. & C. B. Division of C. M. & St. P. Ry. At present is official stenographer of Iowa Banker's Association. Expects to practice in Deadwood, South Dakota. Republican. Permanent address, Deadwood, South Dakota.

CHARLES H. MATTINGLY, ... SPRINGFIELD, OHIO.

Prepared for college at Olney, Illinois. Before entering Michigan, stenographer and book-keeper. Expects to practice in Detroit, Michigan. Republican. Permanent address, Olney, Illinois.

Albert Eugene McCabe, ... Alanson, Mich.

Born at Alanson, Michigan, March 22, 1866. Before entering Michigan engaged in lumber business. At Michigan; President U. of M. Democratic Club. Democrat. Permanent address, Alanson, Michigan.

Russell Norman McConnell, ... McPherson, Kan.

Attorney-at-Law, Kansas. Born at Woodhall, Illinois, November 22, 1868. Attended McPherson High School. Took special course in McPherson Dunkard College. Before entering Michigan, "Pedagogue." At Michigan: Recording Secretary of Jeffersonian Society; Judge of Kansas Club Court; Secretary of Oratorical Board. Member of Ancient Order United Workmen. Expects to practice in Kansas. Democrat. Permanent address, McPherson, Kansas.

William Stephen McConnell, ... Woodstock, Ill.

Born at Woodstock, Illinois, August 1, 1870. Republican. Permanent address, Woodstock, Illinois.

William Herbert Lee McCourtie, ... Marshall, Mich.

Born at Somerset, Michigan, January 16, 1872. Graduated from Marshall High School, Class of '91. Before entering Michigan engaged in business. At Michigan, member of Michigan Club Court. Member of Knights of Pythias. Expects to practice in Michigan. Democrat. Permanent address, Marshall, Michigan.

James Hugh McDonald, ... Heber, Utah.

One year man. Born at Heber, Utah, January 23, 1866. Before entering Michigan clerk in law office. At Michigan, member of Utah Club Court. Expects to practice in Utah. Permanent address, Heber, Wasatch County, Utah.

Peter McDonald, ... Galena, Ill.

One year man. Born in Jo Daviess County, Illinois, February 28, 1865. Attended German-English College and Dixon College. Before entering Michigan engaged in teaching. Member of K. of P. Expects to practice in Illinois. Permanent address, Galena, Illinois.

Michael Leo P. McLaughlin, ... Detroit, Mich.

Born at Crossingville, Pennsylvania, November 18, 1870. Prepared for college at Crossingville, Pennsylvania. Attended Slippery Rock College, Class of '92. At Edinboro: President Excelsior Society; Secretary Potter Society. At Michigan: Member of Jeffersonian Society; Mechem Debating Society. Expects to practice in Texas. "Single Tax Party." Permanent address, 149 Grand River Avenue, Detroit, Michigan.

Harry Clinton Mehan, ... West Superior, Wis.

Born at Peoria, Illinois, October 27, 1871. Before entering Michigan was engaged as abstractor. At Michigan, member of Webster Society. Permanent address, West Superior, Wisconsin.

JOSEPH FRANKLIN MCGREGOR, ... POROWAN, UTAH.

Attorney-at-Law, Utah. Born at Porowan, Utah, August 16, 1869. Attended Brigham Young Academy, Provo, Utah. Principal of Beaver Stake Academy 1890-91. Before entering Michigan, engaged in farming and cattle raising. At Michigan: President of Utah Literary and Debating Society, [1]; Member of Utah Club Court, [2]. Secretary and Treasurer of Democratic Society of Iron County, Utah. Member of "School Board of Examination" of Iron County, Utah, appointed in 1888. Democrat. Permanent address, Porowan, Iron County, Utah.

CHARLES AUGUSTINE MCKNIGHT, ... GRAND RAPIDS, MICH.

One year man. Born near Grand Rapids, May 16, 1870. Commercial traveler several years before entering Michigan. Prepared for law in Grand Rapids Central High School and in the law office of McGarry, McKnight & Judkins, Grand Rapids. At Michigan: Member of Webster Society and Cooley Debating Club; Corresponding Secretary Democratic Club. Democrat. Permanent address, Grand Rapids, Michigan.

SAMUEL MEDBURY, Δ K E, Φ Δ Φ, Θ N E, ... DETROIT, MICH.

Born at Detroit January 3, 1872 One year with Class of '95, Literary Department, University of Michigan. At Michigan: Assistant Manager Glee and Banjo Clubs 1892-93; Manager Glee and Banjo Clubs 1893-94. Democrat. Permanent address, 45 Alexandrine Avenue, Detroit, Mich.

ALBERT CYRIL MELCHIOR, Δ Ψ, ... ROSEDALE, MISS.

Born in Mississippi August 28, 1872. Attended for three years Ioka Normal Institute. Took Junior Year of Law at University of Mississippi. At Mississippi: Vice-President and Anniversarian of Herman Society. At Michigan, member of Mississippi Club Court. Expects to practice in Chicago. Permanent address, Rosedale, Mississippi.

WILLIAM HENRY MERNER, ... CEDAR RAPIDS, IOWA.

A. B., University of Michigan, 1892. Born in Ontario, Canada, March 30, 1865. Graduated from High School, Cedar Falls, Iowa. Entered University of Michigan, Class of '92. At Michigan: President Alpha Nu, [4]; Vice-President Political Science Association, 1893-94; Executive Committee Oratorical Association, 1892-93; Member of Alpha Nu, Iowa-Nebraska Club Court, Cooley Debating Club. Member of Masonic organizations. Expects to practice in Iowa. Republican. Permanent address, Cedar Falls, Iowa.

HOMER DWIGHT MESSICK, ... NORTH BRISTOL, OHIO.

B. S., Hiram College, 1891. Born in Mercer County, Pennsylvania, 1866. Graduated from Hiram College, Class of '91. Before entering Michigan, engaged in teaching. At Michigan: Member of Jeffersonian Society; Ohio Club Court. Member of I. O. O. F. Expects to practice in Ohio. Democrat. Permanent address, North Bristol, Ohio.

HARRY EUGENE MICHAEL, ... LEAVENWORTH, KAN.

Born at Leavenworth, Kansas, May 27, 1873. Graduated from Leavenworth High School, Class of '92. At Michigan: Member of Webster Society, Missouri Club Court, Kansas Club Court. Expects to practice either in Chicago, Illinois, or San Diego, California. Permanent address, Leavenworth, Kansas.

JOHN HUBERT MILLER, ... MASSENA, N. Y.

One year man. Born at Louisville, New York, July 7, 1869. Attended the State Normal School, Potsdam, New York. Expects to practice in New York. Republican. Permanent address, Massena, St. Lawrence County, New York.

ALLEN GURNEY MILLS, Κ Σ, ... GEORGETOWN, ILL.

B. S. Earlham College, 1892. Born at Georgetown, Illinois, 1870. Prepared for college in Vermilion Grove Academy. Graduated from Earlham College, Class of '92. At Earlham: Editor of *Earlhamite;* First Price in Oratorical Contest. At Michigan: Member of Jeffersonian Society; Member of Illinois Club Court. Expects to practice in Chicago. Republican. Permanent address, Georgetown, Illinois.

ROBERT EMMET MINAHAN, ... CALUMET HARBOR, MICH.

M. D., Rush Medical College, 1886. Born in New York, January 27, 1858. Graduated from Wisconsin State Normal School, Class of '80. At Normal School, President of Literary Association. At Rush, Vice-President, Class of '86. Practicing physician, 1886–92. At Michigan, President of Law Class of '94. Expects to practice in Wisconsin. Republican. Permanent address, Calumet Harbor, Wisconsin.

HUGH ALBERT MINAHAN, ... OSHKOSH, WIS.

Born at Chilton, Wisconsin, March 24, 1871. Attended State Normal School, Oshkosh, Wisconsin. Before entering Michigan engaged in mercantile pursuits. Member of M. W. A. Expects to practice in Wisconsin. Republican. Permanent address, Oshkosh, Wisconsin.

ROBERT B. MITCHELL, Δ X, ... FREEPORT, ILL.

One year man. Born at Freeport, Illinois, September 8, 1872. Prepared for college at Orchard Lake Military Academy. Attended Beloit College. Expects to practice in Freeport, Illinois. Democrat. Permanent address, Freeport, Illinois.

WILLIS KNOX MOORE, ... BEDFORD, IOWA.

Born at Knoxville, Illinois, July 20, 1868. Before entering Michigan, farming; With Excelsior Milling Company, San Francisco, California, 1890; School teacher, 1891–92. Graduated from Bedford High School, Class of '90. At Michigan: Member of Jeffersonian Society; California Club Court; Nebraska-Iowa Club Court; Vice-President U. of M. Democratic Club. Member of I. O. O. F. Expects to practice in Iowa. Democrat. Permanent address, Bedford, Iowa.

Webster V. Moffett, ... Bloomington, Ind.

A. B., Indiana University, 1889. One year man. Born in Owen County, Indiana, April 22, 1863. Graduated from High School, Spencer, Indiana. Graduated from Indiana University, Class of '89. High School Superintendent, Bloomington, Indiana, 1889-93. Expects to practice in Bloomington. Democrat. Permanent address, Bloomington, Indiana.

J. Monroe Mohnéy, ... New Marysville, Penn.

B. E., Indiana State Normal School, Pennsylvania, 1885. M. E. 1887. Born near New Marysville, 1862. Graduated from Indiana State Normal School, Pennsylvania, Class of '85. At Indiana: Member of A. C. F. W. I. Association. Before entering Michigan: Principal of Ward School, Johnstown, Pennsylvania; Superintendent for two years of Irwin Public Schools, Irwin, Pennsylvania; Editor Irwin *Standard;* For several years immediately preceeding entrance was engaged as a commercial traveller. At Michigan, member of Pennsylvania Club Court. Member of Red Men, Royal Arcanum, Knights of Pythias. Traveled extensively throughout United States and Canada. Expects to practice somewhere in United States. Democrat. Permanent address, New Marysville, Pennsylvania.

Jesse Cameron Moore, ... Delphi, Ind.

Ph. B. Michigan, 1894. One year man. Born at Delphi, Indiana, September 24, 1868. Graduated from Delphi High School, Class of '88. Graduated from Ann Arbor High School, Class of '89. Entered University of Michigan, Literary Department. Attended Harvard University, 1892-93. In law office, 1889-90. In Law School, Winner of Mechem Prize. Expects to practice in Indianapolis, Indiana. Permanent address, Delphi, Indiana.

James Lowry Donaldson Morrison, Σ X, . . Morrisonville, Ills.

Born at Springfield, Illinois, August 2, 1870. Prepared for college at Wyman Institute, Upper Alton, Illinois. Attended St. Mary's College, St. Marys, Kansas. At Michigan: '94 Law Base-Ball Team; '94 Law Foot-Ball Team. Expects to practice in Illinois. Democrat. Permanent address, Morrisonville, Illinois.

Adelbert Mosher, ... Lansing, Mich.

One year man. Born in Macomb County, Michigan, January 1, 1861. Member of Knights of Pythias. Permanent address, Lansing, Michigan.

John Blackwell Newman, Σ A E, ... Elgin, Ill.

M. A. University of Notre Dame, 1891. Born at Elgin, Illinois, November 1, 1870. Graduated from University of Notre Dame. At Notre Dame, 'Varsity Glee Club. Took special work in Literary Department, University of Michigan. In Law School: Member of Illinois Club Court; Member Banquet Committee, U. of M. Democratic Club; Member of Washington's Birthday Committee. Expects to practice in Chicago, Illinois. Democrat. Permanent address, Elgin, Illinois.

Robert Lee Motley, K A, (*Southern Order*), . . Bowling Green, Mo.

A. B. William Jewell College, 1892. Attorney-at-Law, Missouri. Born at New Hartford, Missouri, December 21, 1870. Graduated from William Jewell College, Liberty, Missouri, Class of '92. At Jewell, held various offices in class and literary societies. At Michigan, member of Missouri Club Court. Expects to practice in Missouri. Democrat. Permanent address, Bowling Green, Missouri.

Henry Edmund Naegely, ... Saginaw, Mich.

Born at East Saginaw, March 16, 1869. Prepared for college in East Saginaw High School. Attended Literary Department, University of Michigan, 1889-92, Class of '93. In Law School: President of '94 Law Class, [1]. Expects to practice in Saginaw, Michigan. Democrat. Permanent address, Saginaw, Michigan.

Louis George Nerreter. . . . . Saginaw, Mich.

Born at Saginaw, Michigan, June 27, 1872. In law office before entering Michigan. Expects to practice in Saginaw. Republican. Permanent address, Saginaw, Michigan.

Andrew Richard Nichols, ... Beach City, Ohio.

(No information received).

Byron Lee Oliver, ... Los Angeles, Cal.

Born at Champaign, Illinois, January 12, 1872. Attended Los Angeles High School. Before entering Michigan: Engaged on Santa Fe R. R. Survey in Sierra Nevada Mountains; Survey of Wilson Peak Electric R. R.; "Roughing it" on a California stock ranch in the San Joaquin Valley. At Michigan: Member of Webster Society; California Club Court. Expects to practice in Los Angeles, California. Republican. Permanent address, Union Avenue and 7th Street, Los Angeles, California.

Edwin Calfax Owen, ... White Pigeon, Mich.

(No information received.)

Joseph E. Page, ... Payson City, Utah.

One year man. Born at Payson City, Utah, February 21, 1868. Attended Brigham Young Academy and University of Deseret. Before entering Michigan engaged in dry goods business. At Michigan: Member of Utah Debating Society; Member of Utah Club Court. Expects to practice in Utah. Republican. Permanent address, Payson City, Utah.

Charles Arthur Park, Φ Δ Θ, ... Niles, Mich.

A. B., Wooster University, 1888; A. M., 1891. Born at Niles, Michigan, November 3, 1864. Graduated from Niles High School. Graduated from University of Wooster, Class of '88. At Wooster: Captain of Company B, [3]; President of Class, [4]. Before entering Michigan, Principal of public schools of Fort Morgan, Colorado, 1889-92. At Michigan: Member of Webster Society. Expects to practice in Salem, Oregon. Democrat. Permanent address, Niles, Michigan.

CHARLES DANIEL OREAR, Σ X, ... JAMESTOWN, IND.

Prepared for college in Jamestown High School. Entered DePauw University, Class of '93. At Michigan, Judge of Indiana Club Court. Member of Knights of Pythias. Republican. Permanent address, Jamestown, Indiana.

CHARLES LUCIUS PARKER, ... NEIHART, MONTANA.

A. B., Upper Iowa University, 1881. Born at Fayette, Iowa, August 1, 1859. Graduated from Upper Iowa University, Class of '81. Before entering Michigan, "engaged in farming, speculating, insurance, collecting, private banking." Attended U. of M. Law Department 1889-90. In mining business at Neihart, Montana, 1889-93. Member of I. O. O. F. Republican. Permanent address, Fayette, Iowa.

CHARLES CHANDLER PARKER, Σ Φ, ... FORT SMITH, ARK.

Born at St. Joseph, Missouri, 1872. Prepared for college at Michigan Military Academy. Attended Literary Department University of Michigan, 1891-92. At Michigan: Member of Junior Hop Committee; Sophomore Hop Committee. Republican. Permanent address, Fort Smith, Arkansas.

E. J. PARKER, ... FRANKFORT, MICH.

Born at Parkersburg, West Virginia. Prepared for college in Ferris Industrial School, Big Rapids, and Ann Arbor, Michigan, High School. Engaged in teaching before entering Michigan. Expects to practice at Frankfort. Permanent address, Frankfort, Michigan.

ROBERT STONE PARKS, ... CHARDON, OHIO.

Born at Chardon, Ohio, December 10, 1872. Graduated from Public School of Chardon, 1891. Studied law with Metcalf & King, Chardon, 1891-92. Expects to practice in Ohio. Republican. Permanent address, Chardon, Ohio.

AUGUSTUS ASA PARTLOW, ... DANVILLE, ILL

Born at Danville, Illinois, November 15, 1868. Before entering Michigan, Principal of Lincoln School, Danville, Illinois. At Michigan: First Vice-President of Law Class of '94. Member of K. of P. Expects to practice in Danville, Illinois. Republican. Permanent address, 317 North Hazel Street, Danville, Illinois.

WORTH WILLARD PEPPLE, Σ X,. . . . . LA PORTE, IND.

Born at Indianapolis, Indiana, January 16, 1873. Prepared for college at Michigan City, Indiana. Attended De Pauw University. At De Pauw: Recording Secretary Athletic Association 1889-90; 'Varsity Base Ball Team 1889-90. Attended Literary Department, U. of M., Class of '95. At Michigan: Member of '95 Lit Glee Club 1891-92; '95 Lit Base-Ball Team 1891-92; 'Varsity Base-Ball Team 1891-92. In Law School: Member of 'Varsity Glee Club, [1], [2]; Captain '94 Law Base-Ball Team, [1], [2]; Member of Indiana Club Court. Expects to practice in Indiana. Democrat. Permanent address, 705 Harrison Street, La Porte, Indiana.

HARRY HOWARD PATTERSON, Δ X, ... BEAVER FALLS, PENN.

B. S., Geneva College, 1892. Prepared for college in private and public schools, Beaver Falls. Graduated from Geneva College, Class of '92. At Michigan: Member of Pennsylvania Club Court; Delegate to National Republican College League, Syracuse, New York, [2]. Will probably practice in Beaver Falls, Pennsylvania. Republican. Permanent address, 614 Sixth Street, Beaver Falls, Pennsylvania.

JOHN EVANDER PATTON, ... CHATTANOOGA, TENN.

One year man. Born near South Pittsburg, Tennessee, November 4, 1870. Before entering Michigan, in drug business at Tracy City, Tennessee. Member of K. of P., Royal Arcanum, National Union. At Michigan, member of Webster Society. Expects to practice in Chattanooga. Republican. Permanent address, Chattanooga, Tennessee.

LOUIS PHILIP PAUL, ... MASSILLON, OHIO.

Born at Massillon, Ohio, September 13, 1873. Graduated from East End High School, Massillon, Class of '92. At Michigan: Member of Ohio Club Court; Captain '94 Foot-Ball Team. Does not expect to practice. Democrat. Permanent address, 136 High Street, Massillon, Ohio.

JOHN VINCENT PEARSON, ... PONCA, NEB.

Attorney-at-Law, Nebraska. One year man. Born at Niagara Falls, New York, December 28, 1865. Prepared for college in Fremont Normal School, Fremont, Nebraska, and Preparatory Department, University of Dakota Before entering Michigan, Teacher, Law Student, Clerk of Court of Dixon County, Nebraska. At Michigan, member of Michigan Debating Club. Expects to practice in Nebraska. Democrat. Permanent address, Ponca, Nebraska.

JOHN FURNESS PETERS, ... DETROIT, MICH.

Born at Detroit, Michigan, November 8, 1868. Before entering Michigan, Clerk Legal Department Michigan Central Railroad Company, Detroit. Expects to practice in Detroit. Republican. Permanent address, Detroit, Michigan.

GILBERT W. PHELPS, ... THE DALLES, OREGON.

Born at Mansfield, Tioga County, Pennsylvania. At Michigan: Member of Webster Society; Mechem Debating Club; Columbia River Club Court. Expects to practice in North Dalles, Washington. "Black Republican." Permanent address, The Dalles, Oregon.

CLARENCE ABRAM PLANK, ... LINCOLN, NEB.

One year man. Born at Champaign, Illinois, May 20, 1873. Attended Todd Seminary, Woodstock, Illinois. Before entering Michigan engaged in insurance business and journalism. At Michigan: Member of Webster Society; Benton Debating Club; Nebraska-Iowa Club Court. Expects to practice in Nebraska. Independent in politics. Permanent address, Lincoln, Nebraska.

Edward Scott Pike, ... Chenoa, Ill.

B. S. Illinois College, 1891 Born at Chenoa, Illinois, June 2, 1870. Prepared for college in Chenoa High School. Graduated from Illinois College, Class of '91. Expects to practice in Illinois. Prohibitionist. Permanent address, Chenoa, Illinois.

Edward Dwight Pomeroy, ... Crystal Lake, Ill.

Born at Crystal Lake, Illinois, October 11, 1872. Graduated from Crystal Lake High School, Class of '92. At Michigan: Member of Mechem Debating Society; Illinois Club Court. Expects to practice in Chicago. Republican. Permanent address, Crystal Lake, Illinois.

Clarence Eugene Pope, ... Du Quoin, Ill.

B S. Eureka College, 1891. Attorney-at-Law, Illinois. Born at Du Quoin, Illinois, September 28, 1871. Graduated from Eureka College, Class of '91. At Eureka, won five mile championship gold medal for bicycle race. At Michigan, member of Illinois Club Court. Member of J. O. U. A M. Expects to practice in Du Quoin, Illinois. Democrat. Permanent address, Du Quoin, Illinois.

David Eugene Porter, ... West Burke, Ver.

One year man. Born at Oskosh, Wisconsin. July 16, 1872. Graduated from St. Johnsbury Academy, Vermont, 1892. Teacher, 1892–93. At Michigan; Member Michigan Club Court, Webster Society. Republican. Permanent address, West Burke, Vermont.

James Leonard Poston, ... Netawaka, Kan.

A. B. Washburn College, 1892. Born at Netawaka, Kansas, October 4, 1871. Graduated from Netawaka High School. Graduated from Washburn College, Class of '92. At Washburn: President Gamma Sigma Literary Society; First Honor Gamma Sigma Annual Prize Debate; First Honor in Declamation, 1891; First Honor Kansas State Oratorical Contest, 1892. On Geological Survey for Washburn College, 1887. Is not allied to any political party. Permanent address, Netawaka, Jackson County, Kansas.

John Ward Powers, K Σ, ... Louisville, N. Y.

Born at Louisville, New York, November 19, 1869. Graduated from Potsdam State Normal School, Class of '91. Engaged in teaching before entering Michigan. At Michigan: President of Student's Lecture Association, [2]; Member of Jeffersonian Society, Empire Club Court. Expects to practice in New York State. Republican. Permanent address, Louisville, New York.

Charles Arthur Pratt, ... Traer, Iowa.

B. Ph. Oskaloosa College, 1890. Born at Traer, Iowa, September 13, 1868. Graduated from Oskaloosa College, Class of '90. Before entering Michigan engaged as teacher in Public Schools. Expects to practice in Iowa. Democrat. Permanent addres, Traer, Iowa.

Vanvorhis Alley Powell, ... California, Penn.

Master of Elements, Pennsylvania Southwestern State Normal College, 1888. Born at Coal Center, Washington County, Pennsylvania. Prepared for college in California Public Schools. Attended Pennsylvania Southwestern State Normal College, Class of '88 At P. S. S. N. C., President of Clionian Literary Society; Orator of Class of '88. Took Junior year of law at U. of M., 1889-90. Member of I. O. O. F. Expects to practice in Pittsburgh, Pennsylvania. Republican. Permanent address, California, Washington County, Pennsylvania.

James Dowling Putnam, ... Elmwood, Ill.

Born at St. Paul, Minnesota, March 13, 1859. Before entering Michigan engaged in hotel business; Tobacco Manufacturer; Police Magistrate of the City of Elmwood for seven years. Expects to practice in Elmwood, Illinois. Republican. Permanent address, Elmwood, Illinois.

William Goodpaster Ramsey, Β Θ Π, Φ Δ Φ, . . . Owingsville, Ky.

Attorney-at-Law, Kentucky. Born at Owingsville, Kentucky, December 30, 1871. Prepared for college in Denver High School. Graduated in Historical Science from University of Virginia, Class of '92. Before entering Michigan Justice of Peace, First Magisterial District, Kentucky; Teacher in Public Schools. Member of Masonic Orders and K. of P. Expects to practice either in Colorado or Kentucky. Democrat. Permanent address, Owingsville, Kentucky.

Palmer Seymour Reavill, ... Ann Arbor, Mich.

Born at Flat Rock, Illinois, February 6, 1868. Prepared for college in Preparatory Department of De Pauw University. Before entering Michigan, Farmer, Stockdealer and Village Clerk. Member of I. O. O. F. Expects to practice in Utah or Illinois. Democrat.

Guy Leonidas Reed, Κ Σ, ... Butte City, Mont.

Born at Mexico, Missouri, September 4, 1873. Prepared for college at Phillips Exeter Academy. Attended William Jewell College, Class of '92. At Michigan: President Mechem Debating Club; Member of Webster Society; Illinois Club Court; Oregon Club Court. Expects to practice in Montana. Democrat. Permanent address, Butte City, Montana.

Benjamin Franklin Reed, ... Metamora, Mich.

One year man. Born at Metamora, Michigan, May 13, 1874. Prepared for college in Lapeer, Michigan, High School. Before entering Michigan was in law office of Judge S. B. Gaskill, of Lapeer, for two years. At Michigan; Member of Jeffersonian Society, Michigan Club Court. Expects to practice in Detroit, Michigan. Democrat. Permanent address, Metamora, Michigan.

Charles Howard Rector, ... Helena, Mont.

Permanent address, Helena, Montana.

JUDSON ELIAS RICHARDSON, ... REED CITY, MICH.

Son of E. S. Richardson, M. D., Michigan '70. Born at Saginaw, Michigan, July 29, 1872. Graduated from Reed City High School, Class of '89. Engaged in teaching, 1889-92. At Michigan: Secretary Webster Society; Secretary U. of M. Prohibition Club; Vice-President Michigan Inter-Collegiate Prohibition Association. Prohibitionist. Permanent address, Reed City, Michigan.

HEDLEY VICARS RICHARDSON, Φ Δ Φ, ... DETROIT, MICH.

Ph. B University of Michigan, 1893. Born at Tendell, Ontario, Canada, 1870. Graduated from Detroit High School, Class of '89. President and Class Prophet D. H. S., Class of '89. Graduated from University of Michigan, Class of '93. At Michigan: Chairman Arrangement Committee Freshman Banquet, [1]; Member 'Varsity Glee Club, [1], [2], [3], [4]; President 'Varsity Glee and Banjo Clubs, [4]; Reception Committee Senior Reception, [4]; Toast Master '93 Banquet, [5]. Member of Lowell Club, Detroit. Expects to practice in Detroit. Republican. Permanent addres, Detroit, Michigan.

LULU BUFFINGTON RICHARDSON, ... PITTSBURGH, PENN.

A. B. Granville College, 1892. Born at Columbus, Ohio, September 13, 1872. Graduated from Granville College, Class of '92. Attended Law School of University of City of New York. At New York; Vice-President of Law Class of '94. At Michigan: Second Vice-President of Law Class of '94; Director of Students Lecture Association.

VICTOR HOWARD RINGER, Σ N, Φ B K, ... WILLIAMSPORT, IND.

Ph. B. DePauw, 1893. Born at Williamsport, Indiana, February 13, 1870. Prepared for college in Williamsport High School. At De Pauw; Associate Editor of *De Pauw Mirage*, [3]. Took Junior year of Law at De Pauw. Republican. Permanent address, Williamsport, Indiana.

FRANK A. ROCKHOLD, ... DETROIT, MICH.

One year man. Born at Canton, Illinois, January 26, 1869. Graduated from High School, Kansas City, Missouri. Attended University of Nebraska, Class of '93. Before entering Michigan was Private Secretary to the Pacific Coast Manager of the Standard Oil Company, San Francisco, California. Expects to practice at Omaha, Nebraska. Democrat. Permanent address, Omaha, Nebraska.

HENRY THEODOR RONNING, ... GLENWOOD, MINN.

Born in Pope County, Minnesota, January 28, 1869. Attended St. Cloud Normal School, Minnesota. Before entering Michigan engaged in teaching; Studied Law with C. J. Gunderson, Law '85, Alexander, Minnesota, 1891-2. At Michigan: Member of Webster Society; Indiana Club Court. Expects to practice in Minnesota. Republican. Permanent address, Glenwood, Minnesota.

HUGH EMERSON ROOT, ... MASON, MICH.

One year man. Born at Lansing, Michigan, July 3, 1872. Graduated from Mason High School. Attended Union University. Expects to practice in Mason. Democrat. Permanent address, Mason, Michigan.

DANIEL LINDSAY RUSSELL, Δ K E, Φ Δ Φ, ... WILMINGTON, N. C.

Attorney-at-Law, North Carolina. One year man. Born at Wilmington, North Carolina, November 18, 1870. Graduated from Cape Fear High School, Wilmington, North Carolina. Attended Quakenbush Boarding School, Laurinburg, North Carolina. Attended the University of North Carolina. In law office of Judge D. L. Russell, 1890-93. At Michigan, Member of Webster Society. Expects to practice in Detroit, Michigan. Republican. Permanent address, care Dr. F. H. Russell, Wilmington, North Carolina.

SAMUEL MCNEAL SCHALL, ... MANORVILLE, PENN.

Born at Blanket Hill, Pennsylvania, October 25, 1865. Attended Edinboro Pennsylvania State Normal School; Greenway Seminary. Before entering Michigan engaged as teacher for five years. At Michigan; Member of Pennsylvania Club Court; Assistant Marshall, Class of '94. Member of I. O. O. F. Expects to practice in West Virginia. "Randal Democrat." Permanent address, Manorville, Pennsylvania.

OREON EARLE SCOTT, ... BETHANY, W. VA.

A. B. *Summa cum laude*, Bethany College, 1892. Born at McClellandtown, Pennsylvania, November 11, 1871. Prepared for college in public schools. Graduated from Bethany College, Class of '92. At Bethany: Secretary Neotrophian Literary Society, [1]; Business Manager *Bethany Collegian*, [4]; President Neotrophian Literary Society, [4]; Greek Orator Senior Class, [4]; Financial Agent Bethany College, Summer of '92. At Michigan: Member Washington Birthday Committee, [1]; Editor *U. of M. Daily*, [1]; Treasurer Mechem Debating Club, [2]; Marshal Jeffersonian Society, [2]; Business Manager TO WIT: [2]; Invitation Committee, Michigan Press Association Banquet, [2]; Chairman Committee on Commencement Invitations for Senior Law Class, [2]; Member of Missouri and Indiana Club Courts. Member of Royal Arcanum. Publisher of Students' Directory of University of Michigan, 1893. President of Inland League 1893-94. Expects to practice in the West. Republican. Permanent address, Bethany, West Virginia.

RAYMOND GILMORE SCOTT, B Θ Π, ... BETHANY, W. VA.

A. B. *Summa cum laude*, Bethany College, 1892. Born at McClellandtown, Pennsylvania, December 11, 1872. Graduated from Bethany College, Class of '92. At Bethany: Secretary American Lit.rary Institute, [1]; President American Literary Institute, [4]; Business Manager *Bethany Collegian*, [4]; Pitcher Base-Ball Team, [4]. At Michigan, Pitcher '94 Law Base-Ball Team. Assessor of Taxes, Bethany, West Virginia. Expects to practice in St. Louis, Missouri. Republican. Permanent address, Bethany, West Virginia.

BERTRAM SHANE, ... WARSAW, IND.

Born at Warsaw, Indiana, October 3, 1872. Graduated from Warsaw High School, Class of '90. Before entering Michigan, in mercantile pursuits. At Michigan, member of Indiana Club Court. Expects to practice in Warsaw for two or three years. Permanent address, Warsaw, Indiana.

JAMES J. SHERIDAN, Φ Δ Φ, ... GRAND RAPIDS, MICH.

Attorney-at-Law, Michigan. One year man. Born at Gold Hill, Nevada, August 16, 1868. Prepared for college in public schools of Marshall, Michigan, and Grand Rapids. Before entering Michigan, Assistant Manager, Grand Rapids Veneer Works. At Michigan: Member of Webster Society; Executive Committee U. of M. Republican Club; President U. of M. Republican Club, 1894. Expects to resume practice in Grand Rapids. Republican. Permanent address, Grand Rapids, Michigan.

REUBEN DANIEL SILLIMAN, ... ST. PAUL, MINN.

(No information received.)

EDWIN WALTER SIMS,. . . . . WEST BAY CITY, MICH.

Born at Hamilton, Canada, June 4, 1870. Prepared for college at West Side Academy, West Bay City, Michigan. Before entering Michigan; Newspaper Reporter at Bay City, City Editor *West Bay City Post.* At Michigan: Vice-President '94 Law Class, [1]; President Mechem Debating Society; Vice-President U. of M. Republican Club, [2]; Chairman Michigan Organization; Prosecuting Attorney Michigan Club Court; Member of Webster Society; Member of U. of M. House of Representatives; Executive Committe TO WIT: Board of Editors; Member of Programme Committee Washington's Birthday. Correspondent *Detroit Journal.* Member of K. of P. Secretary of West Bay City Republican Club. Expects to practice in West Bay City. Republican. Permanent address, West Bay City, Michigan.

RUFUS F. SKEELS, ... HOLTON, MICH.

Attorney-at-Law. One year man. Born at Holton, Michigan, March 2, 1872. Attended Flint Normal College and Business Institute, Ferris Business College at Muskegon, Michigan. Expects to practice at Muskegon, Michigan. Republican. Permanent address, Holton, Michigan.

FRED WILBUR SMITH, ... NILES, MICH.

Born at Niles, Michigan, September 1, 1871. Graduated from Niles High School, Class of '91. At Michigan, Member of Webster Society. Member of F. & A. M. Republican. Permanent address, Niles, Michigan.

GEORGE WILLIAM SMITH,. . . . . MANKATO, KAN.

Born at Caledonia, Iowa, May 23, 1870. Prepared for college in Manhattan, Kansas. One year at Kansas State Agricultural College. Member of Sons of Veterans. Republican. Permanent address, Mankato, Kansas.

HUGH CRANES SMITH, Σ X, ... TRENTON, MO.

Born at Trenton, Missouri, April 17, 1873. Graduated from Trenton High School, Class of '91. With C. R. I. & P. R. R. Engineering Corps, 1892. Attended Rose Polytechnic Institute, Terre Haute, Indiana, Class of '95. At R. P. I., Member of Class Base-Ball Team. At Michigan, Member of Missouri Club Court. Expects to practice in St. Louis, Missouri. Woman Suffragist. Permanent address, Trenton, Missouri.

ELLIOTT SPALDING, B Θ Π, ... BROOKFIELD, MO.

Born at St. Catherine, Missouri. Attended State University of Missouri. Expects to practice in St. Joseph, Missouri. Democrat. Permanent address, Brookfield, Missouri.

SHERMAN CLARK SPITZER, Δ X, ... ELGIN, ILL.

B. L. Michigan, 1893. Born at Bloomingdale, Illinois, February 2, 1871. Prepared for college in Elgin High School. Graduated from University of Michigan, Class of '93. At Michigan: 'Varsity Base Ball Team, [2], [3], [4]; Class Base Ball Team, [2], [3], [4]; President Athletic Association, [4]; Financial Secretary Athletic Association, [3]; Director Athletic Association, [3], [4]; Secretary and Treasurer Political Science Association; Toast '93 Banquet, [4], [5]; Orator Senior Class, [4]; *U. of M. Daily* Editor, [4]; Vice-President Students Lecture Association. Republican. Permanent address, Elgin, Illinois.

FRANCIS MARION SPRINGER, ... DANVILLE, IND.

Born in Rush County, Indiana, March 29, 1867. Completed Commercial, Surveying, Engineering and Teachers courses at Central Normal College, Danville, Indiana. Completed Surveying and Engineering courses in Northern Indiana Normal College, Valparaiso, Indiana. Attended Southern Indiana Normal School, Mitchell, Indiana. Took Junior year of Law at Central Normal College, Danville, Indiana. Before entering Michigan, County Surveyor of Rush County, Indiana, 1890–92. Taught school, 1887–90. Republican. Permanent address, Moscow, Rush County, Indiana.

CLARENCE CLAUD STEARNS, ... ATTICA, IND.

Born at Williamsport, Indiana. Prepared for college in Preparatory Department of De Pauw University. Before entering Michigan, engaged in farming and teaching. At Michigan: Member of Webster Society; Indiana Club Court. Member of Knights of Pythias. Expects to practice at Williamsport, Indiana. Republican. Permanent address, Williamsport, Indiana.

CHRISTIE ALFONZO STEARNS, ... JACKSON, MICH.

Born at Jackson, Michigan, March 30, 1873. Republican. Permanent address, Jackson, Michigan.

HARRY LINDLEY STEARNS, ... JACKSON, MICH.

Born at Jackson, Michigan. Member of F. A. M. Permanent address, Jackson, Michigan.

LENN L. STEVENS, ... EUGENE, OREGON.

A. B. University of Oregon, 1892. Born at Eugene, Oregon, November 26, 1869. Graduated from University of Oregon, Class of '92. At Michigan, member of Columbia River Club Court. Expects to practice in Oregon. Democrat. Permanent address, Eugene, Lane County, Oregon.

JAMES ZEBLUON STEWART, JR., ... LOGAN CITY, UTAH.

Born at Draperville, Salt Lake County, Utah, March 6, 1872. Attended Brigham Young College. Before entering Michigan, Principal of Coveville District Schools. At Michigan: President of Utah Literary and Debating Society; Vice-President of Mechem Debating Club. Expects to practice in Logan City, Utah. Democrat. Permanent address, Logan City, Utah.

JOHN GROVER STONE, Β Θ Π, Φ Δ Φ, ... MARQUETTE, MICH.

Born at Allegan, Michigan, September 29, 1871. Prepared for college at Beloit Academy. Attended Beloit College, Class of '95. At Beloit; President of '91 B. C. A. Freshman Banquet Committee; Prize Declamation, [1]. Expects to practice in Michigan. Republican. Permanent address, Marquette, Michigan.

GEORGE RUTHORN STONE, ... HIGH YATE, ONT.

(No information received).

LEWIS AUGUSTUS STONEMAN, Σ X, ... INDIANAPOLIS, IND.

Born at Indianapolis, September 7, 1868. Prepared for college in Indianapolis High School. Before entering Michigan engaged in mercantile and abstract of title business. Will probably practice in Indianapolis. Republican.

JOHN E. SWANGER, ... MILAN, MO.

Attorney-at-Law, Missouri. One year man. Born at Milan, Missouri, January 22, 1864. Attended Kirksville State Normal School. Before entering Michigan, engaged as Teacher in Public Schools; Superintendent of Public Schools of Princeton, Missouri; Representative in the 37th General Assembly of Missouri; Alternate Delegate to National Republican Convention at Minneapolis, June, 1892; Chairman of Congressional Committee of Second Congressional District of Missouri. At Michigan: Member of Webster Society; Missouri Club Court. Member of A. F. & A. M. Expects to practice in Missouri. Republican. Permanent address, Milan, Missouri.

RALPH PERCY TANNEHILL, ... ALLEGHENY, PENN.

(No information received.)

CHARLES H. TINDALL, ... SHELBYVILLE, IND.

Attorney-at-Law, Indiana. Born at Shelbyville, October 12, 1871. Took junior year of law at De Pauw University. At De Pauw, President of Law Class of '93, [1]. In practice at Shelbyville, Indiana, 1892–93. At Michigan: Member of Indiana Club Court. Expects to resume practice in Shelbyville. Republican. Permanent address, Shelbyville, Indiana.

JOHN CHARLES TOBIAS, ... WILSON, KAN.

Born at Elysian, Minnesota, November 15, 1869. Graduated from Wilson, Kansas, High School, Class of '90. For the two years previous to entering Michigan, on a farm near Wilson, Kansas. At Michigan, Member Kansas Club Court. Expects to practice in Wilson, Kansas. Democrat. Permanent address, Wilson, Kansas.

McKENZIE ROBERTSON TODD, K Σ, ... FRANKFORT, KY.

Attorney-at-Law, Kentucky. Born at Madison, Indiana, November 30, 1870. Before entering Michigan, Manufacturer of Confections. At Michigan: Member of Jeffersonian Society; Southern Club Court; Delegate of U. of M. Republican Club to National Republican League Convention at Louisville, May, 1893. Will practice "perhaps in Kentucky." Member of K. of P. Republican. Permanent address, Frankfort, Kentucky.

CHARLES HENRY TOWLE, ... CHICAGO, ILL.

B. L., Michigan, 1892. Born at Omaha, Nebraska, January 11, 1871. Graduated from University of Michigan, Class of '92. Republican.

JULIUS CURTIS TRAVIS, K Σ, ... LA PORTE, IND.

Born at La Porte, Indiana, July 31, 1868. Graduated from La Porte High School. Attended University of Michigan, Class of '92. At Michigan: Business Manager *U. of M. Daily*, [3], [4]. In Law School: Member of Indiana Club Court; Marshall of Law Class of '94; Delegate to National Convention of American Republican College League held at Louisville, Kentucky, May, 1893; Delegate to National Republican Convention at Louisville, Kentucky, 1893; National Secretary of American Republican College League, 1893-94; Executive Committee U. of M. Republican Club, [2]. Member of K. of P.; K. O. T. M. Expects to practice in "the South." Republican. Permanent address, La Porte, Indiana.

DUDLEY CLIFFORD TRUE, ... JACKSON, MICH.

Born at Jackson, Michigan, September 16 1871. Graduated from Jackson High School, Class of '92. At Michigan: Member of Mechem Debating Club; Michigan Club Court. Member of K. of P. Expects to practice in Ohio. Democrat. Permanent address, Jackson, Mich.

EDWARD JAMES TWISS, ... PORT HURON, MICH.

(No information received.)

HENRY CASIMER VIDAL, ... DENVER, COL.

A. B., College of Sacred Heart, 1890; B. S., University of Paris, 1892. Born at Mazamet, Carn, France, December 6, 1873. Graduated from College of Sacred Heart, Denver, Colorado, Class of '90; Graduated from University of Paris, France, Class of '92. At Michigan, Member of Columbia River Club Court. Expects to practice in Colorado. Permanent address, Denver, Colorado.

ARTHUR JOSEPH VINSON, ... JOLIET, ILL.

One year man. Born at Wheatland, Will County, Illinois, September 27, 1867. Attended Plainfield, Illinois High School, and Jennings Seminary, Aurora, Illinois Expects to practice at Joliet, Illinois. Republican. Permanent address, Joliet, Illinois.

JOHN JOSEPH VLACH, ... MENOMINEE, MICH.

Born in Bohemia, Europe, April 6, 1867. Prepared for college in Menominee Public Schools. Before entering Michigan, engaged in "studying, teaching, traveling, and farming." Came to America in 1885. At Michigan: Associate Judge and Clerk of Michigan Club Court; Member of Webster Society; Benton Debating Club; Kansas Club Court. Expects to practice "somewhere in Upper Peninsula of Michigan." Democrat. Permanent address, Menominee, Mich.

LUTHER OGDEN WADLEIGH, Δ K E, Φ Δ Φ, Θ N E, C. & C., . POTSDAM, N. Y.

Ph. B. Syracuse University, 1892. Born at Potsdam, New York, December 2, 1862 Prepared for college at Potsdam State Normal School. Graduated from Syracuse University, Class of '92. At Syracuse: Held various class offices; Calculus Orator; 'Varsity Base Ball Team. Expects to practice in New York State. Republican. Permanent address, Potsdam, New York.

JOHN THOMAS WAGNER, ... IRONBRIDGE, PENN.

A. B. Ursinus College, 1892. Born at Hamburg, Pennsylvania, January 26, 1866. Graduated from Ursinus College, Class of '92. At Ursinus; President of Schaff Literary Society; Society Orator. Before entering Michigan engaged in teaching. At Michigan: Member of Jeffersonian Society; Pennsylvania Club Court. Lecturer to Teacher's County Institutes in various Counties of Pennsylvania. Expects to practice in Norristown, Pennsylvania. "Free Trader out and out." "Believes all tariff is legal robbery." Permanent address, Ironbridge, Montgomery County, Pennsylvania.

JOHN DELISLE WALKELY, ... PONTIAC, MICH.

Born at Stratton, County of Cornwall, England, 1870. Before entering Michigan engaged as Commercial Traveller. Expects to practice in Texas. Democrat.

HENRY C. WALTERS, ... ESSEX, ONT.

Born at Lac La Hache, British Columbia, Canada, August 24, 1870. Prepared for college in Essex High School, Class of '88. Before entering Michigan, Publisher of *Essex Free Press.* At Michigan: President Canadian Club; President Mechem Debating Society; Member of Michigan Club Court; Member University Press Club; Assistant Editor for Law Department of *Michigan Law Journal;* Editor TO WIT: Expects to practice in Detroit, Michigan. Permanent address, Essex, Ontario, Canada.

HENRY WILLIAM WEBBER, ... DENVER, COL.

Permanent address, Denver, Colorado.

Frank Walters, ... Essex, Ont.

Born at Lac La Hache, British Columbia, Canada, March 21, 1865. Prepared for college in Essex High School, Class of '87. Before entering Michigan, Telegraph Operator and Agent M. L. S. & W. Ry.; In Newspaper Business. At Michigan; Assistant Managing Editor, *U. of M. Daily;* Secretary Canadian Club; Member Michigan Club Court; Member Mechem Debating Society; Member University Press Club. Expects to practice in Michigan. Permanent address, Essex, Ontario.

Charles Eugene Ward, Κ Σ, ... Du Quoin, Ill.

Attorney-at-Law, Michigan, Illinois. Born at Du Quoin, Illinois, April 26, 1873. Graduated from Du Quoin High School, Valedictorian Class of '91. Before entering Michigan, Expert Accountant. At Michigan: Member of Webster Literary Society; Illinois Club Court. Expects to practice in Chicago. Independent in politics. Permanent address, Du Quoin, Illinois.

George Fullington Waters, ... Cambridge, Ver.

Born at Johnson, Vermont, November 1, 1867. Engaged in teaching before entering Michigan. Graduated from Johnson State Normal School of Vermont, Class of '88. Expects to practice in Vermont. Republican. Permanent address, Waterville, Vermont.

Adolph Weinberg, ... Augusta, Ill.

Born at Augusta, Illinois. Attended Knox College, Galesburg, Illinois. At Knox; Captain of Foot Ball Team, 1892–93. At Michigan, member of Illinois Club Court. Expects to practice in Illinois. Democrat. Permanent address, Augusta, Illinois.

Edward McKenzie Wellman, ... Elba, Neb.

Born at Viola, Iowa. Attended Western Normal College, Shenandoah, Iowa, and Fremont Normal School, Fremont, Nebraska. Before entering Michigan, Principal of the Public Schools of Elba, Nebraska. At Michigan: Member of Webster Society; Griffin Debating Club; Nebraska-Iowa Club Court. Expects to practice in Omaha, Nebraska. Democrat. Permanent address, Elba, Nebraska.

James Horatio Westcott, Jr., ... Wilmington, Del.

Prepared for college at Ulrich's Preparatory School, Bethlehem, Pennsylvania. Attended Lehigh University, Class of '93. Permanent address, Wilmington, Delaware.

William Erastus Wheeler, Jr., ... Edwardsville, Ill.

One year man. Born at Edwardsville, April 23, 1872. Attended Edwardsville High School; Ann Arbor High School; Literary Department, U. of M.; Literary Department, University of Virginia. At Virginia; Member 'Varsity Glee, Banjo and Mandolin Clubs, 1892–93. Expects to practice in Edwardsville, Illinois. Democrat. Permanent address, Edwardsville, Illinois.

BARTLETT WILEY, Χ Ψ, ... LANSING, MICH.

Born at Lansing, Michigan, November 20, 1868. Prepared for college at Michigan Military Academy. Attended University of Notre Dame, Class of '87. Before entering Michigan was engaged as Newspaper Reporter. Democrat. Permanent address, Lansing, Michigan.

CHARLES OREN WILLITS, Σ Χ, ... KOKOMO, IND.

Ph. B. DePauw, 1894. One year man. Born at Greentown, Indiana, October 9, 1866. Graduated from Greentown High School. Graduated from DePauw University. At DePauw; Vice-President Oratorical Association, [1]; Editor of *DePauw Weekly*, [2]; President of DePauw Athletic Association, [3]; Member of Executive Committee Indiana Inter-Collegiate Athletic Association, [3]; Member DePauw Literary Society. Member of The Skulls, Kappa Phi, Omicron Kappa. At Michigan, member of Indiana Club Court. Expects to practice in Indiana. Republican. Permanent address, 186 South Meridian Street, Kokomo, Indiana.

PERCY WILSON, Θ Δ Χ, Φ Δ Φ, ... FORT MISSOULA, MONT.

A. B. Princeton, 1892. Born at Fort Clark, Texas, January 10, 1872. Attended Macalester College, St. Paul, Minnesota. Graduated from Princeton, Class of '92 Republican.

DANIEL HEISTER WINGERT, ... HAGERSTOWN, MD.

Born at Hagerstown, Maryland, February 13, 1871. Prepared for college in Washington County High School. Attended Harvard University, taking special work in history and political economy. At Harvard, member of Executive Committee of Harvard Union Debating Society. At Michigan: Member of Jeffersonian Society; Treasurer of '94 Law Class, [1]; Marshall of Class, [2]; Member of Reception Committee Second Annual Banquet of U. of M. Democratic Club. Expects to practice in Hagerstown, Maryland. Democrat. Permanent address, Hagerstown, Maryland.

BENJAMIN FRANKLIN WOLLMAN, ... KANSAS CITY, MO.

Born at Leavenworth, Kansas, January 20, 1872. Prepared for college in Kansas City High School. Attended Literary Department, U. of M., 1890–92. In Law School; Member Missouri Club Court; Member Washington Birthday Committee, [1]; Reception Committee Democratic Club Banquet, [1]; Secretary of *Wrinkle*, [2]; Assistant Business Manager TO WIT. Expects to practice in Kansas City. Democrat. Permanent address, Kansas City, Missouri.

WALTER WELLINGTON WOODBURY, Θ Δ Χ, ... JEFFERSON, OHIO.

Born at Jefferson, Ohio, June 19, 1871. Attended Jefferson Educational Institute. Attended University of Michigan, Class of '95. At Michigan: Member of '95 Glee Club; '95 Base-Ball Team. In Law School: '94 Base-Ball Team; 'Varsity Glee Club 1893–94. Expects to practice in Youngstown, Ohio. Republican. Permanent address, Jefferson, Ohio.

John Wright, ... Tuscon, Arizona.

Born at Denver, Colorado, January 29, 1872. Prepared for college at Fordham, New York. Attended University of Notre Dame, Class of '91. Expects to practice at Phoenix, Arizona. Republican. Permanent address, Tuscon, Arizona.

Harry Fralick Worden, Α Δ Φ, Φ Δ Φ, Θ Ν Ε, . Grand Rapids, Mich.

Born at Grand Rapids, Michigan, October 31, 1871. Graduated from Grand Rapids High School. Attended University of Michigan, Class of '94. At Michigan: Toastmaster Freshman Banquet, [1]; Member of 'Varsity Glee Club, [1], [2], [3], [4]; Member of 'Varsity Banjo Club, [1], [2]; 'Varsity Glee and Banjo Clubs, Librarian, [1], Secretary and Treasurer, [2], President, [4]. In Law School: Washington Birthday Celebration, Chairman Music Committee, [1], Member Music Committee, [2]; Member of Campbell Club Court. Delegate to 61st Convention of Alpha Delta Phi. Expects to practice in Grand Rapids. Republican. Permanent address, Grand Rapids, Michigan.

Harry Leroy Yartin, ... Jackson, Mich.

Born at Jackson, Michigan, September 14, 1873, Graduated from Jackson High School, Class of '92. At Michigan: Member of Michigan Club Court; Mechem Debating Society. Expects to practice in California. Democrat. Permanent address, Jackson, Michigan.

George Frederick Zimmerman, ... Mt. Vernon, Ind.

Attorney-at-Law, Indiana. Born at Mt. Vernon, Indiana, January 19, 1870. At Michigan, Treasurer '94 Law Class. Expects to practice in Indiana. Republican. Permanent address, Mt. Vernon, Indiana.

John William Zuber, ... Antwerp, Ohio.

Born at Antwerp, Ohio, May 2, 1873. Prepared for college in Antwerp High School. Graduated from Toledo Business College, Toledo, Ohio, Class of '90. Before entering Michigan, Bookkeeper. At Michigan, Member of Ohio Club Court. Will probably practice at Antwerp, Ohio. Democrat. Permanent address, Antwerp, Ohio.

Former Members.

Cooley Cash Anderson,	Midland, Mich.
Delbert Martin Bader,	Detroit, Mich.
Clarke Edward Baldwin,	Adrian, Mich.
Daniel Robertson Barlow,	Mahaney City, Penn.
Thomas Reynolds Best, A. B., *Centre College,*	Millersburg, Ky.
George VanDusen Candler,	Detroit, Mich.
Archibald Cattell, Jr., A. B., *Iowa College,*	Davenport, Ia.
John Conrick,	Chamberlain, S. Dak.
June Wallace Cory,	Saginaw E. S., Mich.
Lester McDonnell Coulter,	Lindsay, Ont.
Sylvanus Wright Curtiss, Jr., Ph. B., *Michigan,*	Monroe, Mich.
Joseph Benjamin Dabney,	Chicago, Ill.
Hamilton Fitzgerald Dobbin,	Altoona, Fla.
Oliver James Dolan,	Peoria, Ill.
James Noble Dunham,	Paola, Kan.
Horace Levi Dyer,	St. Louis, Mo.
Albert Eugene Felmley, B. S., *Iowa State Normal College,*	Cedar Falls, Ia.
Ernest Linwood Finley, A. B., *University of Wooster,*	Mt. Pleasant, O.
John Kinney,	Joliet, Ill.
Fred Alexander Forsythe, B. L., *Washington and Lee University,*	Harrodsburgh, Ky.
Jesse Carl Foulks,	Topeka, Kan.
Thomas Frank Fulkerson,	Trenton, Mo.
Oscar Charles Garrett,	Elsie, Mich.
William Henry Harrison Garver,	Monticello, Ill.
John Edwin Gilmore,	Weeping Water, Neb.
Horace Cadwell Gordon,	Grand Rapids, Mich.
Henry Killmaster Gustin,	Killmaster, Mich.
Samuel Jesse Hall,	Augusta, Mich.
George Jacob Haller,	Ann Arbor, Mich.
Pleasant Stephen Harris,	Adel, Ia.
Robert Terrell Harris,	Ogden, Utah.

Elmer Maxwell Hayden, A. B., *Iowa College*,	Tacoma, Wash.
Virgil White Hill, A. B., *South West Kansas College*, ...	Augusta, Kan.
Jay LeRoy Hitchcock, ...	Pontiac, Mich.
Jesse Huber, ...	Bluffton, O.
Joseph Wesley Humphrey, ...	Bryan, Ont.
William Louis Ireland, ...	Chesaning, Mich.
Isaac Thomas Jones, ...	Cantril, Ia.
Hiram Scott Joslin, ...	Anamosa, Ill.
John Henry Killmaster, ...	Killmaster, Mich.
Gordon Nathan Kimball, ...	Ogden, Utah.
Hector Mahlon King, ...	Axtell. Kan.
Miles Lintlater.	Jackson, Mich.
Andrew Watson Lockton, ...	Marshall, Mich.
Edward Reed Loud, A. B., *Albion College*, .	Albion, Mich.
William Nicholas Marshall, ...	Unionville, Mo.
Henry Arnaud McCormick, ...	Salt Lake City, Utah.
Andrew McCardell, ...	Salt Lake City, Utah.
Lewis Charles O'Conner, ...	Geneseo, N. Y.
Walter Dartt Peters, ...	Green Bay, Wis.
Fenimore Cooper Packett, ...	Detroit, Mich.
George Egbert Pyatt, ...	Betheny, Ill.
Dennis Patrick Quinlan, ...	Ishpeming, Mich,
Allen Holbrook Reynolds, ...	Walla Walla, Wash.
Arthur White Richardson, ...	David City, Neb.
Lewis Rinaker, B. S., *Blackburn University*, .	Carlinville, Ill.
Elmer Elton Roland, B. S., *Franklin College*, .	Franklin, Ind.
William Walton Shier, ...	Detroit, Mich,
Frank Linden Smith, ...	Carbondale, Penn.
Harry Porter Stearns, B. S., *Michigan*, .	Adrian, Mich.
Francis Adams Stivers, ...	Liberty, Ind.
James Taylor, ...	Fort Branch, Ind.
Henry William Trash, ...	Butte City, Mont.
Arthur J. Tuttle, Ph. B., *Michigan*, . .	Leslie, Mich.
James Walton, ...	Northfield, Mich.
Philip Henry Waters, ...	Detroit, Mich.
James J. Welsh, A. B., *Lombard University*, .	Williamsfield, Ill.
John Frank Wilkeson, ...	Buffalo, N. Y.
Royal Melville Williamson, ...	Kansas City, Mo.
William Nelson Woodland, ...	Oneida, Idaho.
Octavius John Charge Wray, ...	Red Jacket, Mich.

Class Statistics.

MEMBERSHIP, ... 289
FORMER MEMBERS, ... 71
ATTORNEYS-AT-LAW, ... 32
AVERAGE AGE, ... 24 yrs 8 mo.
OLDEST MAN—Robert Emmet Minahan, born January 27, 1858.
INFANTS—Eugene Batavia, born August 8, 1873; Rex Ronald Case, born August 10, 1874; Benjamin Franklin Friend, born August 11, 1874; Edwin Charles C. Hennings, born January 20, 1875; Charles Albert Bull, born February 23, 1874; Charles Edgar Cochran, born May 8, 1873; Matthew Francis Coleman, born August 3, 1873; George Jacob Genebach, born June 29, 1874; Fred Hosea Hathhorn, born August 12, 1873; William John Landman, born July 23, 1873; John Adolph Lentz, born April 20, 1874; Harry Eugene Michael, born May 27, 1873; Louis Philip Paul, born September 13, 1873; Clarence Abram Plank, born May 20, 1873; Guy Leondias Reed, born September 4, 1873; Benjamin Franklin Reed, born May 13, 1874: Henry Casimer Vidal, born December 6, 1873; Harry Leroy Yartin, born September 14, 1873; John William Zuber, born May 2, 1873.

Geographical Distribution.

Michigan,	86	Texas,	3
Illinois,	37	Ontario, Canada,	3
Ohio,	23	Kentucky,	3
Indiana,	19	Tennessee,	2
Pennsylvania,	19	Arkansas,	2
Iowa,	13	West Virginia,	2
Missouri,	9	Washington,	2
Kansas,	8	North Dakota.	2
Utah,	8	Massachusetts,	1
Montana,	6	Wyoming,	1
Nebraska,	6	Maryland,	1
New York,	5	South Dakota,	1

Colorado,	5	Mississippi,	1
Minnesota,	3	Arizona,	1
Wisconsin,	4	North Carolina,	1
Oregon,	4	Delaware,	1
California,	4	Japan,	1
Vermont,	3		

Class Politics.

Republican,	122	Single Tax,	1
Democrat,	94	"Black Republican,"	1
Prohibitionist,	9	"Democrat *in Sempiternum*,"	1
Independent,	6	Undecided,	37
Woman Suffragist,	1		

Degrees.

A. B.,	28	B. E.,	3	M. D.,	1
B. S.,	16	M. E.,	3	B. C. E.,	1
Ph. B.,	12	A. M.,	2	B. S. D.,	1
B. L.,	4				

Members of Greek Letter Fraternities.

Φ Δ Φ,	17	Σ N,	3	Σ A E,	2
Σ X,	12	Δ K E,	3	A Δ Φ,	1
Δ X,	9	Σ Φ,	2	X Ψ,	1
K Σ,	8	Θ Δ X,	2	Δ Ψ,	1
B Θ Π,	7	Z Ψ,	2	Δ Υ,	1
Δ T Δ,	6	Φ K Ψ,	2	Φ A Π,	1
Θ N E,	5	Φ Δ Θ,	2	A T Ω,	1
Ψ Υ,	4	K A (S. O.),	2	Φ B K,	1

Faculty of Law.

JAMES B. ANGELL, LL. D.,
President.

LEVI T. GRIFFIN, A. M.,
Fletcher Professor of Law.

BRADLEY M. THOMPSON, M. S., LL. B.,
Jay Professor of Law.

JEROME C. KNOWLTON, A. B., LL. B.,
Marshall Professor of Law.
DEAN.

JOHN W. CHAMPLIN, LL. D.,
Professor of Law.

FLOYD R. MECHEM,
Tappan Professor of Law.

ALEXIS C. ANGELL, A. B., LL. B.,
Professor of Law.

OTTO KIRCHNER,
Professor of Law.

*ANDREW C. McLAUGHLIN, A. B., LL. B.,
Advanced Course in Constitutional Law and Constitutional History.

HERMAN V. AMES, Ph. D.,
Lecturer on Constitutional Law.

THOMAS C. TRUEBLOOD, A. M.,
Professor of Elocution and Oratory.

ELIAS FINDLEY JOHNSON, B. S., LL. M.,
Instructor in Law.

THOMAS M. COOLEY, LL. D.,
Lecturer on Inter-State Commerce.

HENRY H. SWAN, A. M.,
Lecturer on Admiralty.

VICTOR C. VAUGHAN, Ph. D., M. D.,
Lecturer on Toxicology and its Legal Relations.

MARSHALL D. EWELL, LL. D., Chicago, Ill.,
Non-Resident Lecturer on Medical Jurisprudence.

SAMUEL MAXWELL,
Justice of the Supreme Court of Nebraska, *Non-Resident Lecturer on Code Pleading and Practice.*

*Absent on Leave.

JAMES L. HIGH, LL. D., Chicago, Ill.,
Non-Resident Lecturer on Injunctions and Receivers.

MELVILLE M. BIGELOW, Ph. D., Boston, Mass.,
Non-Resident Lecturer on Insurance.

JOHN B. CLAYBERG, LL. B., Helena, Mont.,
Non-Resident Lecturer on Mining Law.

RICHARD HUDSON, A. M.,
Lecturer on Comparative Constitutional Law.

GEORGE H. LOTHROP, Ph. B.,
Non-Resident Lecturer on Patent Law.

HENRY C. ADAMS, Ph. D.,
Lecturer on the Railroad Problem.

WILLIAM G. HAMMOND, LL. D., St. Louis, Mo.,
Non-Resident Lecturer on History of the Common Law.

JOSEPH H. VANCE, LL. B.,
Law Librarian.

Assistants to the Professors of Law.

JOHN W. DWYER, LL. M.
THOMAS W. HUGHES, LL. M.

Board of Regents.

Hon. HERMANN KIEFER, ... *Detroit.*
Hon. ROGER W. BUTTERFIELD, ... *Grand Rapids.*
Hon. CHARLES HEBARD, ... *Pequaming.*
Hon. LEVI L. BARBOUR, ... *Detroit.*
Hon. WILLIAM J. COCKER, ... *Adrian.*
Hon. PETER N. COOK, ... *Corunna.*
Hon. HENRY HOWARD, ... *Port Huron.*
Hon. FRANK W. FLETCHER, ... *Alpena.*

JAMES H. WADE,
Secretary and Steward.

HARRISON SOULE,
Treasurer.

President James B. Angell, LL. D.

NO NAME in educational circles is probably better known, both in America and abroad, than that of James Burrill Angell, LL. D., President of the University of Michigan. He was born in the town of Scituate, Rhode Island, on the 7th day of January, 1829. He is directly descended from Thomas Angell, who came from Massachusetts into Rhode Island with Roger Williams.

His early education was obtained in the common schools of his native town. Later, for the period of two years, he was a pupil in academies in Seekonk, Massachusetts, and in North Scituate, Rhode Island. This was followed by a like period, in work on his father's farm. He finished his preparation for college in the University Grammar School in Providence, chiefly under the instruction of Dr. Henry Simmons Frieze, who was later president of the University of Michigan. He entered Brown University as a freshman in September, 1845. Among his contemporaries in college were Hon. S. S. Cox, Justice Durfee, of Rhode Island, Rev. Dr. Fisher of Yale Theological Seminary, Judge Dickman, of Cleveland; Rev. Dr. Murray, dean of Princeton College, and the late Professor Diman. He graduated in 1849 with the highest honors of his class.

The first year after graduation was spent as an assistant in the University library, at the same time giving private instruction to students. The next winter was spent travelling through the South on horse back for his health, which, upon his return, was so precarious that it was thought necessary for him to lead an outdoor life He decided, therefore, to take up civil engineering and spent some months in this work. But in December, 1851, he gave up engineering and started on a trip to Europe.

Soon after arriving there he received an invitation from the trustees of Brown University to take the chair of modern languages or the chair of civil engineering. He chose the former, but remained in Europe till August, 1853, travelling and studying in Italy, France and Germany. He filled the chair of modern languages and literature in Brown University until 1860 with the most gratifying success, during which time he wrote a great many leading articles published in the Providence Journal. In 1860 he was given the whole editorial care of this paper, which position he occupied for six years.

Professor Angell was now offered the presidency of the University of Vermont, which position he accepted, and was inaugurated in August, 1866. In 1869 the degree of LL. D. was conferred upon him by his Alma Mater— the highest honor she could bestow upon one of her sons. Within this same year he was invited to take the position of president of the University of Michigan, but declined because he felt he could not properly leave the Vermont University at that time; but, however, the invitation having been tendered two years later, in 1871, he concluded to accept. This brought Dr. Angell to Ann Arbor, to the head of the leading educational institution in the West.

Dr. Angell is not only an educator of renown but is a well recognized diplomat as well. In 1879 the President of the United States appointed him Minister to China. This

PRESIDENT JAMES B. ANGELL.

was in no sense a political appointment. It was an appointment eminently fit to be made; a proper recognition of a learned, polished and refined gentleman. The manner in which Dr. Angell performed his duties as the representative of the United States government at Peking, in effecting a settlement of the then existing international differences, was very satisfactory to the President of the United States, as well as to the entire people.

In 1887 Dr. Angell was again honored by President Cleveland. He, together with Thomas F. Bayard, then Secretary of State, and the Hon. William L. Putnam, now judge of the United States Circuit Court, of a New England circuit, were appointed by the President as plenipotentiaries of the United States to act in conjunction with the Rt. Hon. Joseph Chamberlain, Lord Sackville and Sir Charles Tupper, the British plenipotentiaries, This commission was appointed for the purpose of negotiating a settlement of the differences then existing between the United States and Great Britain, concerning the rights and privileges of American fishermen in the ports and waters of British North America.

This commission met in November, 1887, and formulated a treaty and reported it to the President on the 15th of February, 1888, but did not finally finish its labors until October of the same year.

When Dr. Angell assumed the Presidency of the University of Michigan there were about a thousand students in the institution. The cares growing out of the great responsibilities of his station have not prevented him from making his influence felt throughout the entire country.

"His addresses on literary and educational topics; his generous and elegant hospitality to all Alumni and friends of the University; his earnest, Christian sympathy, as shown in his baccalaureate discourses to students; his happy methods of keeping in harmony the various elements of the different faculties; his genial firmness as a disciplinarian, together with his remarkable familiarity with the condition and wants, as well as the weaknesses of individual students, exerts a powerful and permanent influence in behalf of higher education in Michigan and throughout the Northwest."

Dr. Angell was married in 1855 to Sarah S. Caswell, daughter of the late President Caswell of Brown University. They have three children.

Dr. Angell's life has been a very busy one. Besides answering the many calls upon his time, by reason of his position as President, he has contributed numerous articles to the leading reviews and magazines, all indicating the profound scholarship and thought of their author.

Of all the persons with whom the thousands of students of the University come in contact while here none are longer remembered or more beloved than is President Angell.

Dean Jerome C. Knowlton.

PROF. JEROME C. KNOWLTON was born at Plymouth, Wayne County, Michigan, December 14, 1850. His parents were descendents from that sterling stock of New England, which has furnished so many of the great and noble men who have peopled the Northwest. His early life was spent upon a farm near South Lyons, Michigan, where, while in the free and open communion with nature, he fostered that love of books and zeal for knowledge which have so characterized him in his manhood. In 1867 he matriculated in the State Normal School, but entered the High School of Ann Arbor in the fall of the same year, completing this course in 1870. He matriculated in the fall of 1870 in the classical course in the University of Michigan; was obliged to leave college at the end of his Freshman year on account of ill health, for one year, but re-entered in fall of 1872 and graduated with the class of 1875 with the degree of A. B.

While in college he was considered the foremost scholar of his class, being decidedly proficient in the classics and English literature. He was distinguished in the debates of the college societies and in the field of college journalism. Professor Knowlton was selected by his class to make the commencement speech. He was recognized as a student of marked ability and promise. He entered the Law Department in 1876, and graduated in 1878, and immediately entered the law office of the Hon. A. J. Sawyer, of Ann Arbor, with whom

DEAN JEROME C. KNOWLTON.

a co-partnership was formed a year later under the firm name of Sawyer & Knowlton. In 1882 he was commissioned postmaster at Ann Arbor by President Arthur. Three years later he was appointed an assistant professor in the Law Department and was given charge of the recitation work; while so engaged he edited the second American edition of "Anson on Contracts" in 1887, which is the standard text-book in the law schools of the country. Prof. Knowlton was appointed Marshall Professor of Law in 1889, and was made acting dean in October, 1890, upon the resignation of Professor Rogers, and dean the following June. The Board of Regents were exceedingly fortunate in securing a man who is as well qualified for the position of Dean of the greatest law school in the world to-day, as all the students who have come under his supervision will testify. Although a young man, he already occupies a high position at the bar.

Prof. Knowlton possesses great strength of mind; has great capacity to seize upon the vital points of the controversy and an instinctive command of general principles. Judge Cooley has said of him that, "he was one of the best lawyers in the State." The most intricate problems of law are easily unravelled and become lucid through his arguments. His rhetoric and logic, both in manner and form, are perfection. He has contributed a great number of articles for the leading Law Journals of the country, which indicate his thorough knowledge of the fundamental principles of the law. His special subjects in the department are: Contracts, Bailments and Carriers, Criminal Law, Criminal Procedure and The Law of Railways. In September, 1875, Prof. Knowlton was married to Miss Adelle M. Pattengill, who, appreciating his aspirations, has ever been an inspiration as well as his companion in success.

Hon. Levi T. Griffin.

OF THE many eminent lawyers in the State of Michigan, none have achieved greater prominence at the bar, as practitioners, than Professor Levi T. Griffin. It has been said of him that he has perhaps tried more cases than any other lawyer in the State. It is certain that his clientage has been large, and his practice extensive and lucrative.

He was born in Clinton, Oneida County, New York, May 23, 1837. His father, a gentleman of refinement and culture, especially noted for his social qualities, inherited a considerable landed estate, which was conveyed to his paternal ancestors in 1790 by George Washington, whose signature, with that of De Witt Clinton as a witness, is upon the title deed. His parents came to Michigan in 1847.

At the age of sixteen Professor Griffin entered the University of Michigan. Here he maintained a good position in his classes, and was proficient in all his studies except mathematics, which he never examined sufficiently to appreciate. After graduating in 1857, he entered the office of Moore & Blackmar, of Detroit, as a law student. Through the exertions of Mr. Moore, a distinguished member of the bar, then assistant United States district attorney, he secured the appointment of court deputy. With this financial assistance, he was able to get through the first year of his study. During this time he was accustomed to sleep in the office on a bed improvised for the occasion. He was admitted to the bar May 29, 1858. After a few months he removed to Grand Rapids and associated himself with Lucius Patterson, for some years one of the best known lawyers of Western Michigan. Here he remained until 1860, when he returned to Detroit and resumed his connection with Moore & Blackmar, where he remained until 1862, at which time the partnership of Moore & Griffin was formed.

He entered the army in the autumn of '62 as a commissioned officer, and continued in the service until mustered out July 1, 1865, having been brevetted major of volunteers for gallant and meritorious services. He belonged to the famous Fourth Michigan Cavalry, the regiment that captured Jefferson Davis at the close of the war. His reputation with the regiment was that of an able and gallant officer.

Returning after the close of the war, he again entered on the practice of the law, and in 1865 associated himself with Hon. Don M. Dickinson. Professor Griffin has been eminent in the counsels of his political party, and was nominated by it in 1887 as a candidate for justice of the Supreme Court of Michigan, but was defeated by that honored jurist of Michigan, Hon. James V. Campbell.

After the resignation of Mr. Kent, Fletcher professor of law in the University of Michigan, Professor Griffin was appointed his successor by unanimous vote of the Board of Regents, which position he still holds.

In the fall of 1893 Professor Griffin was nominated and elected as the representative in Congress of the First Michigan District.

Professor Griffin is a man of pronounced individuality and indefatigable industry. His special subjects are "Evidence," "Federal Jurisprudence," "Common Law Pleading," and "Personal Property."

HON. LEVI T. GRIFFIN.

Prof. Bradley M. Thompson.

THE subject of this article was born April 16, 1835, at Milford, in the then Territory of Michigan. He prepared for Wesleyan College, but matriculated in the University of Michigan in 1854, graduating in the Literary Department in 1858, and in the Law Department in 1860 with the first class. He began the practice of his profession at East Saginaw in 1860; formed a partnership with the Hon. William L. Webber and Judge Chauncey H. Gage in the spring of 1862; in the fall of '62 he entered the United States service as captain in the Seventh Michigan Volunteer Cavalry. This regiment was brigaded with the First, Fifth, and Sixth Michigan cavalry regiments, and was known as Custer's Brigade, being in command of that gallant officer.

Professor Thompson was mustered out of the service in 1865 as brevet colonel, for gallant and meritorious services. He held the office of city attorney of East Saginaw during the years '73, '74 and '75, and the office of mayor for two terms during the years 1877 and 1878. In 1878 he was the candidate of his party for Congress in the triangular contest in which Hon. R. G. Horr and Hon. H. H. Hoyt were the other candidates, all being residents of the same city and ward. He carried his county by a large majority, but R. G. Horr was elected. In 1880, there being a vacancy in the office of circuit judge in the Tenth Judicial Circuit, composed of Saginaw County, at a meeting of the bar of that court Professor

PROF. BRADLEY M. THOMPSON.

Thompson was recommended to the governor of the State as the choice of the bar for that office.

In 1887 the Board of Regents of the University appointed him to deliver a course of forty lectures on the subject of Real Property, and at a meeting of the Board in June following he was made Jay Professor of Law. In 1893 he was elected mayor of the City of Ann Arbor.

In private life, Professor Thompson is genial, open-hearted and hospitable. In conversation he is brilliant and instructive. Among all classes he is most highly respected. He is a man to whom the people can go, and do go for counsel with the full assurance of a careful hearing and of the right kind of assistance. "In his speech he is methodical, correct, rounded and concise; his critical analysis of subject covers all its points and leaves no gaps to fill."

Professor Thompson is enthusiastically interested in true professional education; his style is clear and pointed. He has been in the active practice of the law for the past thirty years, and his practice has extended to all the courts of the State and United States.

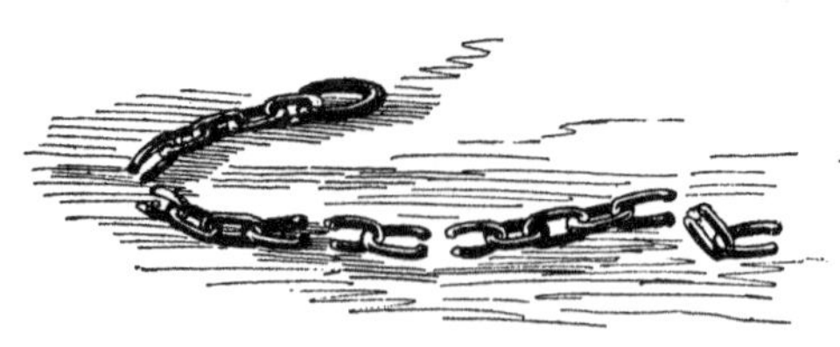

Prof. Floyd R. Mechem.

PROFESSOR MECHEM was born in the State of New York on the 9th of May, 1858. His parents removed to Michigan when he was a small boy. He was at an early age, by force of circumstances, obliged to depend upon his own efforts for his support, and at times worked upon a farm, kept books, and while attending the high school in Ann Arbor, from which he graduated, drove a delivery wagon in order to pay his way. He taught several terms of school, spending his evenings reading law, and was admitted to the bar at Marshall, Mich., in 1879, at once entering into partnership with his preceptor Mr. Wadleigh, and began practice at Battle Creek, Mich. Afterwards he formed the firm of Hulbert & Mechem; then F. R. & G. W. Mechem; then Mechem Hulbert & Mechem. This last firm had probably the best business in the County. Professor Mechem at this time had a large trial practice in the counties surrounding Calhoun. He was four times City Attorney of Battle Creek, and in 1882 declined the nomination for Prosecuting Attorney of Calhoun County, Mich., on account of his valuable practice. He removed to Detroit, Mich., in 1887, where he soon was a recognized leader at the bar. He here formed the firm of Mechem & Beaumont. He has tried several important cases, in both the highest courts of the State and Nation.

At about the time he went to Detroit he began to write books which gradually absorbed most of his time. He is the author of "Mechem on Agency," "Mechem on Public Officers," "Mechem's Hutchinson on Carriers," "Mechem's Leading Cases on Agency"; besides many legal articles published in the leading Law Journals of the United States, and which are marked by a legal acumen, extended research, a familiarity with the authorities and a sound logic, which have gained the favorable opinion of the legal fraternity generally. His works are widely quoted as authority upon their respective subjects. He organized the "Detroit College of Law." He was called to the chair of Tappan Professor of Law in the Law Department of the University of Michigan in 1891. It has been said of him by those most familiar with his method of work, that "in temperament, in methodical industry and in facility of analysis he resembles Judge Cooley." He has charge of the "Practice Court" which has attracted so much attention during the past year. His work in this court is highly praised by all. His special subjects in the department are "The Science of Jurisprudence," "The Law of Domestic Relations," "Agency," "Partnership," "Wills, Their Execution and Revocation," and "The Administration and Distribution of Estates of Deceased Persons."

He married the only daughter of the Honorable V. P. Collier, of Battle Creek, former State treasurer of Michigan, and two children brighten the home of Professor and Mrs. Mechem.

6 PROF. FLOYD R. MECHEM.

Judge John W. Champlin.

AMONG the men of prominence and distinction in the history of Michigan during the last quarter of a century, the name of John W. Champlin stands in a place of deserved and honorable prominence. The traits of mental power and honesty of character which have made Judge Champlin so strong with the people of Michigan are the marked characteristics of his ancestors.

Judge Champlin was born February 7, 1831, at Kingston, Ulster County, New York. He is a descendant of Geoffrey Champlin, who in 1638 came to this country from England and settled in Rhode Island. He spent his younger years with his father upon the farm, except when at school, until he was twenty-one years old. He entered the academy of Rhinebeck, Duchess County, New York, at thirteen; later, after completing a course at Harpersfield, he took a course in civil engineering at Delaware Institute, Franklin, New York. He removed to Grand Rapids, Mich., in 1854, where he has since resided and where he commenced reading law in the office with his brother; was admitted to the bar the following year and began the practice of his profession.

In 1857 he was chosen to prepare the charter of the city of his adoption, and the result of his work has been the basis of all the charter legislation of that city. He was at different times city recorder, city attorney, and mayor of Grand Rapids, and thus acquainted himself thoroughly with the workings of

JUDGE JOHN W. CHAMPLIN.

municipal government. Probably there is no lawyer in his part of the State whose opinion is more widely respected upon questions of municipal law than is his. In the trial of cases he was uniformly courteous to the court, his opponent, and to the witnesses. He cared nothing for mere display, always seeking the truth. In 1883 Mr. Champlin was nominated by his party and elected judge of the Supreme Court of this State by a majority far in excess of the vote of his own party. As an official and a citizen his vote and influence have ever been on the side of law and order. As a lawyer he enjoys an enviable and well-earned reputation, possessing not only legal acumen, but brilliancy as an advocate. In his practice, as in his personal life, he is a man of the highest honor and strictest integrity. He was honored with the degree of LL. D. by the University of Michigan in 1887, and was appointed a professor in the Law Department of the University of Michigan in 1892, which position he still holds. He was an excellent judge, and has written many opinions which have been widely quoted. He has been connected with the trial of a great many leading and important cases both in the State and Federal courts. On October 1, 1856, he was married to Miss Ellen Moore, and has been blessed with three children.

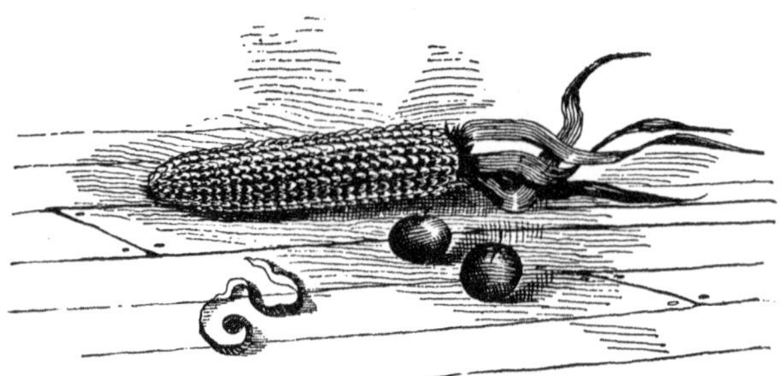

Prof. Otto Kirchner.

PROFESSOR OTTO KIRCHNER is a native of Prussia. He was born at Frankfort on the Oder July 13, 1846; came to the United States in 1854; studied law in Canada and was admitted to the bar of the Supreme Court of Michigan at Detroit, November 10, 1865, and to the bar of the Federal courts the same day. He was clerk of the judiciary committee of the House of Representatives of Michigan during the session of 1865; was elected Attorney-General of the State of Michigan in 1876, and again in 1878, having been nominated each time by his party by acclamation.

He was appointed Kent Professor of Law in the University of Michigan in the fall of 1885, and delivered a course of lectures upon commercial law. He also delivered a course of lectures to students of the law department in the spring of 1891 upon the subject of private corporations. He was again appointed a professor in the fall of 1893, and lectures to the seniors upon "Private International Law" and to the juniors upon "Marital Relations."

Professor Kirchner is a man of a very positive character. He has been engaged in the active practice of the law at Detroit, Michigan, for more than a quarter of a century, during which time he has been connected with the trial of a great many cases of national importance. His practice has extended to the highest courts of both the State and nation.

As a lawyer Mr. Kirchner has attained a very high standing among his contemporaries. He is distinguished for his great integrity, intrepidity, legal erudition and skill, as well as for his faithfulness and untiring industry. He is a close thinker upon all subjects, and a deliberate and careful speaker; and added to these characteristics, a pungent and refined wit.

As a member of the Detroit bar he has won for himself an enviable reputation and wide circle of friends and admirers both among those with whom he has been thrown in contact professionally as well as in the private walks of life. From his first appearance as a regular professor in the Law Department, Professor Kirchner has been a special favorite with the students.

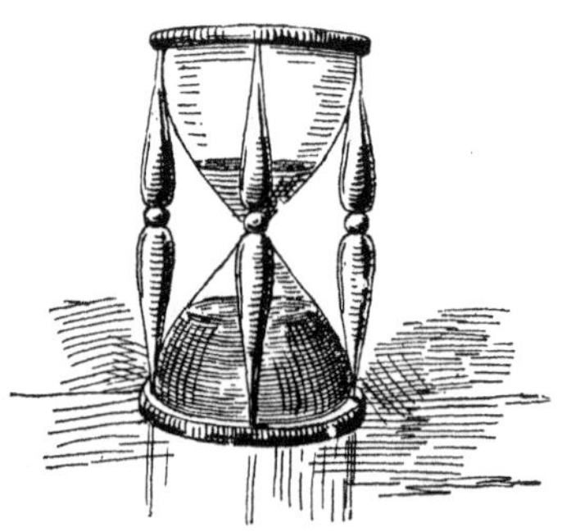

PROF. OTTO KIRCHNER.

Prof. Alexis C. Angell.

PROFESSOR ALEXIS C. ANGELL was born April 26, 1857, at Providence, Rhode Island, where he resided until 1866, when he removed to Burlington, Vermont, and later to Ann Arbor in 1871. He graduated from the Literary Department of the University of Michigan with the degree of A. B. in 1878; read law during 1878–79 with the firm of Walker & Kent, of Detroit, and was admitted to the Detroit bar in the latter year. He entered the Law Department of the University of Michigan as a student in the fall of 1879, and graduated the following June with the degree of LL. B., and at once commenced the practice of his chosen profession in Detroit. He became a member of the firm of Wells, Angell, Boynton & McMillan in June, 1892.

He edited the last editions of "Cooley's Constitutional Limitations," "Cooley's Constitutional Law," and "Cooley on Torts." He has also written several articles for the leading journals of the country. He was called to the Law Department after the very sudden death of Professor W. P. Wells in 1891 to finish the course of lectures on Constitutional Law. In the fall of 1893 he was again appointed to a professorship in the department where he lectures on Constitutional Law and Domestic Relations.

He has been connected with the trial of many important suits in the highest courts of his State and the United States. He married Miss Cooley, daughter of Judge T. M. Cooley.

PROF. ALEXIS C. ANGELL.

Hon. Henry B. Brown.

THE University of Michigan Law School is honored by having as one of the members of its faculty a Justice of the Supreme Court of the United States, Henry B. Brown. He was born in Lee, Massachusetts, on the 21st of March, 1836. His father was a manufacturer, and his mother was a woman of exceptional strength of character. He was educated at Yale University, from which he graduated in 1856, with Chauncey M. Depew and his present associate, Mr. Justice Brewer, as classmates. At the close of his college course he spent a year in Europe, studying languages, and travelling extensively on the Continent. Upon his return he pursued a course of study at the Law School of Yale University, but received his degree from the Harvard Law School.

In 1859 he went to Detroit, and there entered the office of a prominent law firm, in which he continued until April, 1861, when he was appointed Deputy United States Marshal and Assistant District Attorney. He held the latter office until 1868, when Governor Crapo appointed him to fill a vacancy in the Wayne Circuit Court, the highest court in the city of Detroit. Returning to the practice of his profession, he formed a partnership with the late J. S. Newberry and Ashley Pond. In 1875 he was appointed by President Grant, District Judge of the United States, succeeding Judge J. W. Longyear, which position he held until the 29th of December, 1890, when he was appointed and commissioned Justice of

HON. HENRY B. BROWN.

the Supreme Court of the United States by President Harrison.

As a practitioner his time was almost exclusively in the United States Courts, and his knowledge of admiralty proceedings, together with his familiarity with the domain of Criminal Law, made him eminent in those branches. As an admiralty judge he has tried a far larger number of cases than any other judge upon the bench, and is a recognized authority in this field, having written a great number of very important opinions.

He was appointed a lecturer in the Law Department of the University of Michigan in 1888, upon the subject of admiralty law, which position he still holds. His perceptive faculties are quick, and he works with facility and ease. The duties of his various positions have been discharged with untiring industry, acknowledged ability and impartiality. His style is clear, emphatic, and at times picturesque.

Prof. Thomas C. Trueblood.

PROFESSOR THOMAS C. TRUEBLOOD is a native of Southern Indiana. He was fitted for college at Blue River Academy; entered Earlham College, from which he received the degree of A. M. Early in life the desire to become a thorough and accomplished public reader and teacher of the arts of Elocution and Oratory was awakened in him. He embraced every opportunity for instruction in these arts. He was persistent in his efforts to acquire the best known methods, and to this end studied with the most distinguished masters in this country and in England, notably the late Mr. James E. Murdoch and subsequently with the late Professor Charles John Plumtree of Kings College, London.

In 1878 he taught a few months in Indiana and later the same year, together with Professor Robert I. Fulton, established the "Fulton & Trueblood's 'School of Oratory,'" in Kansas City, which, in 1882, became a department of the University of Kansas City. In 1884 Professor Trueblood taught in the Universities of Missouri, Kentucky, and in the Ohio Wesleyan University. In 1884 he commenced his work in the University of Michigan, where so much of his time was employed that he was soon obliged to give up all his other work, save at the Ohio Wesleyan, and in 1889 the work at the University of Michigan consumed all his time.

In December, 1892, Professor Trueblood was offered the Chair of Oratory in Princeton College, but the Board of

Regents at about this time promoted him to a full professorship in "Elocution and Oratory," and he decided to remain here. In the summer of 1893 he conducted the Summer School of Elocution and Oratory at Chatauqua, N. Y. Through the efforts of Mr. Trueblood the Northern Oratorical League was founded. He is an earnest advocate of the simple, business-like methods of public address, a style of Oratory of which Wendell Phillips was the first great representative—a dignified, energized, conversational style.

He and his associate, Mr. Fulton, now of the 'Ohio Wesleyan University, have issued a number of publications, the most important of which are "Practical Elements of Elocution," "Choice Readings," "Critic's Tablets," and a "Chart of Vocal Expression." The first named book was issued in September, 1893, and that it is appreciated as a text-book is evidenced by the fact that it is now in its second edition, and has already been introduced in a number of colleges and universities. By his constant work and method of instruction he has aroused an enthusiasm and interest in the subject of Elocution and Oratory, which we feel is not manifested in any of the other great universities of the country, and to his credit, it may be said, that in the three contests already held in the "Northern Oratorical League," composed of the following colleges: University of Michigan, Oberlin College, Northwestern University, University of Wisconsin, Iowa University, and the University of Chicago, his students have won two.

PROF. THOMAS C. TRUEBLOOD

Prof. E. F. Johnson.

PROFESSOR E. F. JOHNSON, son of ex-Judge Abel Johnson, of Ohio, was born at Van Wert, Ohio, on the 24th day of June, 1861. He graduated from the high school in '77, after which he taught several terms. In 1880 he was admitted to the senior class in the University of Ohio; shortly after, deciding to follow the profession of teaching, he entered the National Normal University of Ohio, receiving the degree of B. S. in '81. The same year he was appointed Superintendent of Schools for Van Wert County, which position he resigned in 1883, to accept the Republican nomination for representative of that county. Though Van Wert county was Democratic, Mr. Johnson was elected at the fall election by a large majority, having the honor to be, not only the first Republican representative from the county, but also the youngest member of the legislature. He represented his county until 1887, coming to Ann Arbor in 1888. While at Columbus he read law with Hon. William W. Johnson, Chief Justice of the Supreme Court of Ohio. At Ann Arbor he took the degree of LL. B. in '90, and LL. M. in '91. He has since been connected with the department, and is now instructor in the law of "Extraordinary Remedies," "Commercial Paper," "Criminal and Code Pleading." His method of instruction is eminently practical, as it embodies, so far as may be, not only a drill in the law proper, but in its application as well. He has written several articles for legal journals and also prepared a small work on "How to Teach."

7 PROF. E. F. JOHNSON.

Joseph H. Vance.

ONE of the most obliging men that can be found about the Law Department of the University of Michigan is Joseph H. Vance, the Librarian of this department. Mr. Vance is a native of the State of New Jersey. His people removed to Michigan in 1840, since which time he has been a resident of this state.

He entered the Law Department and graduated in 1861, being a member of the second law class. He immediately engaged in the practice of law at Ann Arbor and continued in the practice until 1883, when he was put in charge of the Law Library, which position he still holds.

In 1890 he edited a very valuable work, "Jurisdiction, Its Exercise in Commencing an Action at Law," which has had a large sale.

JOSEPH H. VANCE.

THE ORIGINAL FACULTY.

CHARLES I. WALKER.

THOMAS M. COOLEY. JAMES V. CAMPBELL.

The Founding of the Law Department of the University of Michigan.

WHEN the Law Department of Michigan University was organized in 1859 the Department of Literature, Science and the Arts had been open for eighteen years. It began in a small way; the Northwest was still for the most part a wilderness, and Ann Arbor, to which it was proposed to invite students, was but a small pioneer village, having accommodations neither for students nor for those who should instruct them. These accommodations must therefore be provided. Forty acres in the village had been given for a University campus, and on the north and south sides of this respectively two houses were erected for the occupation of professors, and the buildings which now constitute the wings of the main structure on the grounds were put up. One of these was given up to the use of students as a dormitory. The Department grew in numbers and strength slowly but steadily, and after nine years had elapsed, the Department of Medicine and Surgery was opened, and a building erected for its accommodation. The Faculty of that Department was one of marked ability, and the school they taught was soon favorably known throughout the country. With the exception of the buildings already noticed the campus in 1859 was an open field, made use of by the students for athletic purposes. The need of dormitories on the grounds had by that time ceased, and the rooms the students had occupied were appropriated to the purposes of instruction. The room then used for a chapel was in the north college building, the university houses were still occupied by professors, though it was not expected this would much longer be the case, and with the exception of the house altered over for the use of the President, and in which he now resides, they have at the time of this writing for several years been appropriated to other purposes.

A Law Department in the University had been in contemplation from early territorial days, and was required by a mandatory provision in the act of 1837 by which the University scheme was very carefully and fully outlined. It would perhaps have been earlier organized, but the means at command were extremely limited, and as the Literary Department was obviously the first necessity it received the first attention. The Law Department was the second named in the act, but when it became possible to go further, the medical men were first on the ground, and without opposition from the legal profession, they secured favorable action from the Regents for the opening of a Medical School. The call for such a school was made evident by the attendance the first year, which was ninety-one.

The question of organizing the Law Department was not taken up until 1858. The Board of Regents had then been reorganized on a new basis: it had before consisted of a body of twelve men appointed by the Governor, with the Governor himself, the Lieutenant Governor, the Judges of the Supreme Court and the Chancelor as *ex-officio* members. It was now composed of ten members chosen by popular vote, one being elected in each of the judicial districts into which the State was divided. A majority of these were lawyers. A law committee was appointed, consisting of J. Eastman Johnson, Benjamin L. Baxter and Donald McIntyre, all of whom were lawyers, though the last named was no longer in practice but had become a banker. At the meeting of the Board in December, 1858, this committee was instructed "to consider and report a plan for the establishment of a Law Department in the University," and it immediately proceeded to do so.

The report was made at the March meeting, 1859, and was taken up, approved and adopted. The general features of the plan were that instruction in the law should be given by three professors to be chosen by the Board, and that it should begin on the first of October following and continue for six months in each year. As there was at the time no building that could be devoted exclusively to the purposes of this instruction, it was proposed that the room then used for a chapel should be made use of for law lectures and other department exercises, and that a library should be purchased for the department which for the time being must find accommodations in the general library room. The annual salary proposed for each professor was one thousand dollars. Such was the scheme. Before adjournment the Board proceeded to the election of the professors, and James Valentine Campbell and Charles Irish Walker, of Detroit, and Thomas McIntyre Cooley, of Adrian, were unanimously agreed upon. The choice was made without, so far as is now known, any previous consultation with the persons selected.

Henry P. Tappan was at that time President of the University and presiding officer of the Board of Regents. He was a man of large ability, commanding presence and good speaking talent, who had been recommended to the place by the historian George Bancroft, to whom it had been first offered, and he had fully proved his fitness not only by instruction given in philosophy and other lines, but also by his skill in administration, and the general good will he had secured from professors and students. Difficulty between himself and the Regents sprung up afterwards which led to his leaving the University, but at this time the relations between him and the Board were altogether harmonious and agreeable. In the matter of planning for a Law Department there is nothing in the records indicating that he took active part, but what was done is known to have had his cordial approval, and he contributed, in so far as his office gave occasion for his doing so, to make the success of the plan complete. And it may properly be added here that so long as he remained president of the University his relations to the Law Department were altogether pleasant and satisfactory.

It may well be called a piece of good fortune that the Regents were able to secure the services of Professors Campbell and Walker for the new school. The salary offered was not attractive, and if either of them accepted, it would be from a sense of duty or from love of the work. They would not be expected to change their residences from Detroit to Ann Arbor, but to go out for the delivery of lectures would be attended with no slight inconvenience. Professor Campbell was then in the prime of life. He was born at Buffalo, N.Y., in 1823, but his father removed with him to Detroit in 1826 while Michigan outside of Detroit was almost an unbroken wilderness, and the small town in which his father took up his abode was still little more than a French village. He had grown up with the town, and as boy and man had always been a favorite with its people. He was admitted to the bar in 1844, and it was not long before he had made for himself a place among its leaders. His legal acquirements were broad and thorough, his mind was acute and clear, he was remarkably quick as well as accurate in his perception of legal principles, he was a forcible though not an eloquent speaker, never attempting to be ornate, but keeping closely to the point in hand, and, from the obvious sincerity and candor with which he urged his views upon court or jury, he had demonstrated his worth as an advocate, and had no difficulty in securing and keeping his full share of professional success. The Supreme Court of the State had just been reorganized on a popular basis, the Justices to be elected in the State at large, and by common consent he seemed to be indicated as eminently fitted for a place in it, and was chosen. Professor Campbell had a taste for historical pursuits, especially as related to his own country, and though he had not up to this time appeared as an author, except of minor articles, he did so subsequently, publishing in 1876 the "Outlines of the Political History of Michigan," an octavo of 600 pages, which has standard value.

Papers and addresses published or made by him at different times, and now recalled to mind, are the following: "The dangers of Church Centralization," 1856; "Moravians in Michigan," 1858; "Some remarks on the Polity of the Protestant Episcopal Church in the United States," 1865; "Our City Schools." Address delivered in Toledo, 1869; "Does the Law deal Unfairly with questions of Insanity," 1870; "Of the taking of Private Property for purposes of Utility," 1871; "Some hints on Defects in the Jury System," 1876; "Law Abridgment," 1879; "Materials of Jurisprudence," 1880; "Judicial History of Michigan." Semi-centennial address delivered at Lansing, 1886.]

He was a modest man, but steadfast in his opinions, and as a Judge had all those qualities we like to see in one who may be called on to determine the legal claims we make, and the rights we undertake to defend as against invasion by others.

Professor Walker was the senior of Professor Campbell by some nine years, having been born in Otsego County, New York, in 1814. He came to Michigan in 1836 when the rage for speculation in wild lands and town sites was fast becoming a mania, and in 1839 he entered upon the study of the law. In 1840 his studies were interrupted by an election to the State Legislature, but after service in that body for one term he decided to go to New England to complete his preparation for the bar. This he did, in part at Springfield, Mass., and in part at Brattleboro, Vt., and after admission to the bar he practiced law in Vermont until 1851. He then returned to Michigan and opened a law office in Detroit. That he might look for distinguished success will be apparent when it is stated that he was thoroughly grounded in legal principles, that his candor and purity of purpose were always unquestioned, that he was noted rather for patient labor and accuracy than for quickness, but that in the give and take of trials and legal contests of all sorts his antagonist seldom found him unprepared or unequipped. He was a gentleman always, and his courtesy was unfailing. He could hardly be called an easy or a graceful speaker, but he always stated his points with clearness and precision, and by close adherence to them commanded the attention of his audience whenever and wherever he spoke. He interested himself greatly in matters pertaining to the early history of the Northwest, and in 1858 he delivered an elaborate and carefully prepared address on "De la Motte Cadillac and The First Ten Years of Detroit," which was followed later by papers on "The Early Jesuits in Michigan," "Michigan from 1796 to 1805," "The Civil Administration of General Hull," and in 1871 he delivered an address before the Historical Society of Wisconsin on "The Northwest during the Revolution." These all have permanent value. No one doubted that Professor Walker would prove an excellent teacher in his new position if he accepted it.

Professor Cooley was youngest of the three appointees, having been born at Attica, N. Y., in 1824. He removed to Adrian in this State in 1843, and there completed law studies which he had been following in New York for a year, and was admitted to the bar in 1846. He was best known to the people of the State at the time of his appointment by the Regents through a compilation he had made and published in 1857 of the General Statutesof the State. Two general revisions of the statutes which had before that time been made had proved unsatisfactory, and the people in amending their constitution had forbidden the making of any more, and had required the legislature to elect a compiler to bring together and publish all general statutes whenever it should be thought needful. The legislature chose Mr. Cooley to do this work in 1857. The task was one of some nicety and difficulty, as it went back to the earliest days of territorial government, but it was completed within the year, and the result in two large volumes had been received with satisfaction by the legislature and the public. The plan of arrangement then made use of has been followed, ever since. The reorganized Supreme Court had made the compiler its official reporter, and he had published one volume of reports, and in 1859 had another nearly ready. It may be added here that his subsequent labors as an author were mainly but not altogether in the line of the law.

The professorships in the Law Department were named, respectively the Marshall, Kent, and Jay professorships, after the great American jurists who bore those names, and Professor Campbell was assigned to the first professorship, Professor Walker to the second, and Professor Cooley to the third.

The new appointees met shortly after the action of the Regents had been taken, and proceeded to consider the situation. A great labor had been thrown upon them, and it became necessary that they should determine the manner in which it should be performed, and assign to each of their number the part he was to take in it. The first necessity obviously was to provide for a resident professor, for none of their number then resided at Ann Arbor. Circumstances seemed to indicate clearly that the resident professor must be the third named on the list, for his residence was at a point that would preclude his retaining it and discharging with any convenience to himself the labors expected from him. No objection was, therefore, made on his part to the desire expressed by the others that he should at once remove to Ann Arbor. The subjects upon which they should respectively give instruction were then brought under discussion. The Regents had not undertaken to apportion these, and the professors, after full consideration, reached an agreement that Professor Campbell must take whatever pertained to Equity Jurisprudence and its administration, to Criminal Law, the Law of Evidence, and Shipping and Admiralty; that to Professor Walker should be assigned Contracts, including Bills and Notes, and Commercial Law generally, together with Common Law Pleading and Practice. This left to Professor Cooley the Law of Real Estate, of the Domestic Relations, and whatever pertained to the Estates of Deceased Persons, Uses and Trusts, and Constitutional Law. The mere statement of these general subjects is sufficient to indicate how great each professor must have felt was the burden that had been put upon him. In making the assignments the professors had, to some extent, consulted personal wishes and taken into consideration what had been the lines of their practice at the bar, and the subjects with which they had most often been called upon to deal, but this could not be altogether controlling, and some subjects, as was to be expected, were accepted rather unwillingly. Nevertheless, the assignments as made were accepted without serious objection, each yielding something to the wishes of his associates. The inadequacy of the time at their command for a satisfactory presentation of the several branches of the law by means of lectures was obvious, the professors felt it very forcibly, and it was agreed between them that, so far as should be found practicable, they must arrange to be always accessible to students, that the instruction given by lectures might be supplemented by that which could be given in their consultation rooms when personal calls were made for assistance or explanation. The purpose expressed to this effect was always acted upon afterwards, and the general fact was that the professor lecturing for the day was really not giving instruction for two lecture hours merely, but for all the time that he remained upon the University grounds.

It is the history of all educational institutions that they are at times greatly pressed for means; and this was emphatically true of the University of Michigan at the time the regents proceeded to establish the Law School. It was then exceedingly difficult for them to meet the current expenses of the University, and they had only acted, in enlarging the field of instruction, upon what they felt to be an imperative obligation, but the salaries paid must be the very smallest that would secure competent performance of the duties, and they were at first fixed at the very inadequate sum already named, because to pay a larger would be impossible.

The place designated for the delivery of lectures, it was agreed on all hands, was an exceedingly unsuitable one. It was not only inadequate for the needs of the department, but its use for that purpose to some extent interfered with uses to which it had been appropriated before. It was only taken for the purpose because no other room was then available, and the regents recognized the necesslty of taking immediate steps looking to provision for better accommodations. For that purpose the law committee of the regents and the law faculty were empowered and requested to devise, if possible, ways and means whereby a suitable building might be erected for the exclusive use of the Law Department. They were also authorized to examine as to the best locality for the building, and to present a general plan therefor to the regents. The committee at once entered upon the performance of this duty, persevered in it until success had crowned their labors.

The general course of instruction in the department was to embrace two lectures of an hour each for five days in each week. Upon these lectures the professor who delivered them examined the class afterwards. The plan adopted for the examination was such as to make the exercise quite as much one of instruction for the student as one calculated to draw from him what he had learned from the lecture upon which he was examined, for it was accompanied continuously by explanations, by remarks additional to what had been said before, by the citation of illustrative cases, and by responses to such questions as the students felt inclined to ask, either upon what the professor had said in the lecture or upon the general subject.

The Law Department was formally opened at the beginning of October, 1859, and Professor Campbell, who had been made Dean of the Faculty, delivered an able and thoughtful address on "The Study of Law." A short extemporaneous address was also made by the President of the University. The number of students entering the department the first year was ninety. Several of these had been admitted to the bar before coming, and a still larger number were fully prepared for admission under the rules then prevailing for the purpose in the circuit courts of Michigan, but had delayed applying therefor that they might first take a law course in the new school. The first law lecture was delivered by Professor Walker. The students who had entered were all very naturally in exuberant spirits, for they partook of the general feeling of exultation that the new department was now to be added to the University. The most of them had personal acquaintance with the new professors, and were gratified by the choice the Regents had made, and when Professor Walker took the lecture stand he was received with a demonstration of noisy exuberance that testified in a very emphatic manner, not only to their good feeling, but also to their satisfaction in coming under his instruction.

Professor Walker was in many respects a model lecturer. He was never in the habit of writing his lectures out, but he spoke from very full notes, presenting the leading principles upon which he proposed to address the class very clearly, though concisely, enlarging upon them as he proceeded, and giving citations to many cases the bearing of which he explained. He had a strong voice. He spoke deliberately, and no one had any difficulty in catching exactly what he said, or in taking copious notes as the lecture proceeded. His general course continued the same so long as he remained in the department. It is almost needless to say that from the very first he was always a favorite with the students, for what he undertook to teach them was clearly and forcibly put, and they could not well fail to understand and retain it. Professor Campbell followed Professor Walker on another lecture day. His course was somewhat different: his notes were more fully written out, and he spoke with great ease and fluency. He covered more ground in a lecture than did his associate who preceded him, and what he said, if written out precisely as delivered, might almost without correction or change have been accepted as a chapter in a standard work upon the subject treated. The writer has often thought that if his lectures upon equity jurisprudence had been taken down exactly as he delivered them, and reproduced in book form, they would have constituted a not inadequate substitute for any work on that subject then in existence. He was not less acceptable to the classes than was Professor Walker, though they followed him with somewhat more difficulty, and took less copious notes of what he said.

Instruction in the Law School was now fairly begun. It was said by one who some years afterwards wrote upon the history of the University, emphasizing in doing so some unpleasant controversies, that the Law Department had no history. By this was meant only that it had no internal dissensions to attract public notice, and no quarrels with other departments, or with their professors, or with the governing authorities of the University. Understood in this sense, the statement is entirely correct. The department had no history of this unpleasant sort. Its business went on peacefully and regularly, with unbroken success, without demonstration of any sort having for its object the annoyance of others, or to give to its own affairs factitious importance or prominence. It should in fairness be admitted, however, that the manner in which the students received their first professor in the lecture room was so enjoyable at the time that it was repeated from day to day, and was soon found to have perpetuated itself: the habit of receiving their preceptors with good-natured but noisy demonstrations whenever they took the lecture stand, and of indulging sportively in similar demonstrations, during any little recess between exercises was never abandoned. But it should also be said that the practice never became discourteous to professors, and no instance is recalled in which it failed to yield when a call to order was made by the lecturer for the day. The demonstration never had for its purpose to insult or annoy; there was simply boisterous good-nature, which resulted in no harm to any one, and was tolerated because it caused no vexation.]

It was agreed by the professors at their first meeting that moot courts must be made a special feature of the course, quite beyond what had been customary in law schools, and that the professors must give freely of their time in assisting the students assigned to take part in them in their preparation for the hearings, This understanding was carried out with liberal expenditure of labor, and the moot courts became an attractive feature in the instruction. The students very generally attended them; they were presided over by the lecturer for the day, who made such suggestions as seemed called for as the argument proceded. At the conclusion he commented upon and criticised the briefs and discussion, if it seemed wise to do so, and then applied the law. By this course he did not simply decide the case that had been discussed, but he gave instruction upon the points involved as well as upon the manner in which the counsel had prepared for and presented them, and made the exercise one of practical value.

The first law commencement took place at the end of March, 1860. Twenty-four of the class were by their attainments deemed worthy to receive the degree of Bachelor of Laws, and it was awarded to them. The day was a gala day, not only to the students themselves, but to the people of Ann Arbor, who flocked to the hall to witness the ceremonies. A new department of the University was now launched, and had been successfully opened. The work for the year had been satisfactory to the Regents, and to every one concerned. It seemed certain that the new department was a success. Justice Isaac P. Christiancy, of the State Supreme Court, a strong man and a profound lawyer, was invited to deliver the commencement address. The address delivered was able, consisting mainly of advice to the young men who were now to enter upon the practical duties of their chosen profession. It was received with enthusiasm by those to whom it was addressed, and was a fitting close to a busy year.

The attendance upon the department for the second year was one hundred and fifty-nine, but in the third year there was a drop to one hundred and twenty-nine. The great civil war was then upon the country, and the young men were rushing to the scene of war instead of to the institutions of learning, where otherwise they might have been looked for. Many who were in the department the year before had now gone to the front, and a number never returned. From this time on, however, attendance in the Law School increased constantly, but the details will not be given here. Students came from all parts of the country, and they scattered after commencement, finding locations in every state and territory of the Union.

The committee who had been appointed by the Regents to select a site for the law building, and to take steps for securing its construction, had been engaged in the performance of their duty from the time of their appointment. In less than three years they were prepared to advise that construction be immediately proceeded with. They selected for the location the spot which was afterward occupied; they secured a plan for the building which was acceptable to the Regents, and in 1862–3 the building was erected and made ready for occupation at the beginning of the law term in October of the last named year. It was thought proper to make the dedication of the building a somewhat notable occasion, and Professor Cooley was designated to deliver an address, and D. Bethune Duffield, the lawyer-poet of Detroit, was invited and consented to enliven the occasion with a poem. The address was largely devoted to pointing out and emphasizing the duties of the lawyer to society, to his profession and to the institutions of his country, and the poem, though much on the same lines, had a special and strong appeal to the patriotic sentiments of those whose profession imposed upon them, more particularly than upon others, the duty, under all circumstances, of abiding by and assisting in the enforcement of the laws of their country, and of supporting by brain, and by life in the last resort, their constitutional government.

As the school continued to grow it was seen by the Regents that its faculty should be enlarged also, and in 1866 provision was made for a new professorship, to be called the Fletcher professorship, this name being conferred in honor of Judge Richard Fletcher of Massachusetts, who had made to the department a valuable donation of books. Mr. Ashley Pond, of Detroit, was appointed to fill it. He was a very able lawyer, and an acceptable lecturer after a manner peculiarly his own. He consented to take the place somewhat unwillingly, His professional business was very large; he was counsel for some very heavy business enterprises, including one of our principal railroads, and after two years' service he felt under the necessity of asking to be relieved. Charles A. Kent, of Detroit, was appointed to succeed him. He also was an able and sound lawyer. His manner, both in the preparation and delivery of his lectures, was not unlike that of Professor Walker; he made his points clearly; he had full notes; he was ready and clear in his explanations, and he secured at once the respect and esteem of his classes, and always retained them. The Tappan professorship, named for the late president of the University, was created in 1879, and Alpheus Felch was chosen to fill it. Professor Felch was one of the best known citizens of the Northwest. He had filled with honor many most important positions; he had been bank commissioner of Michigan when the State was first organized; he had been justice of the State Supreme Court, governor of the State, and senator in Congress, and in every one of these positions he had won honor for himself and commanded the respect of the people. He was now called from his retirement at Ann Arbor to do further service as a teacher of the young men who were to follow him in the profession. He was an excellent lawyer, an easy and graceful speaker, and, though speaking somewhat more rapidly than most of his associates, he made his points so clear that he was followed by his hearers without difficulty, and they were able to take notes sufficiently full for all practical purposes. He resigned his position in 1883, much to the regret of his associates. But Professor Henry Wade Rogers, now president of the Northwestern University at Evanston, Illinois, who was chosen to succeed him, and made dean of the faculty, proved, as was expected, a worthy successor. His preparation was always full; his delivery was clear, deliberate and pointed. He soon became popular with his classes, and when he retired to accept the position offered him at Evanston, which he still fills with success, he did so greatly to the regret of those who had been associated with him in instruction or otherwise while he remained at this University. Jerome C. Knowlton, the present able and popular dean, who had before been giving instruction as assistant professor, was now very properly advanced to the vacant place.

Brief statement will be made here of the further connection of the members of the first faculty with the school they organized. Professor Walker, who had for some time felt himself overworked, resigned in 1876, and William P. Wells, of Detroit, was appointed to succeed him. Mr. Wells was a good lawyer, and a strong, clear and forcible speaker. Mr. Walker gave lectures in 1879–81 and 1886–87, and then left the school finally. He had well earned his rest. Professor Campbell died in 1890—a great loss to the University and to the state, both of which he had served long, faithfully and ably. Mr. Walker and himself had given valuable instruction in the law to an army of young men, but in no way had their connection with the University and with the department been more important or more useful than in their every-day life and deportment. They were always accessible to proper calls; they met every one courteously, and with no assumption of superiority, and they maintained at all times the dignity of deportment of upright and honorable gentlemen. It hardly need be said that the lesson of such lives is of the very highest value to young men, and that it seldom fails tc have great weight in moulding the character and elevating the motives of those who in youth are fortunate enough to be associated with and impressed by them.

Professor Cooley, from the weight of other duties, in 1884 felt obliged to resign, and his resignation was accepted. From time to time thereafter, however, he found opportunity to deliver lectures upon special subjects, mostly of a constitutional nature, but sometimes upon other topics that for the time had immediate importance. He gave one course upon the Inter-State Commerce Law. This was intended to be a very full and complete course. He also lectured upon Rights, discussing the subject in all its aspects so far as it could be supposed interesting or specially important to a class of law students; also upon legal and constitutional questions involved in municipal government.

In the year 1870 women were received in the classes, and thereafter were always present. The first woman was graduated in 1871. In 1884 the law term was extended to nine months in a year, and in 1886 the classes were separated for the purposes of instruction. In 1889 a post-graduate course was established, upon which attendance has been good. In 1892 a large addition was made to the law building. But the history of the department after the writer left it should be written by some one to whom its interior workings are more familiar. The historical notice he proposed was of the early period only, and is now completed.

The writer will not do full justice to his feelings in regard to the treatment of the department by others connected with the University if he fails to speak of the successive presidents and their cordial relations to the law work. President Tappan has already been spoken of; his successor, Erastus Otis Haven, was equally cordial; so was Henry Simmons Frieze, who for a time was acting president. No one of these took special part in the action of the law faculty, or went beyond lending countenance to what had been decided upon, and their aid in giving it practical effect. President James Burrill Angell has sometimes gone somewhat further: he has many times been the judicious adviser as well as the executive officer, and his aid has been cordially welcomed whenever changes in the *personnel* of instructors, or in the course of instruction, were under consideration. Long may the faculty have the assistance of his wise counsel!

The Law Department of Michigan University has always been in a high sense what its founders meant it should be—a truly national school. We cannot enlarge upon this topic here. One or two facts will sufficiently show the national character of the school. The graduating class of 1890 collected statistics recently which showed members of the class located for business in Arizona, Arkansas, California, Colorado, Delaware, Florida, Illinois, Indiana, Iowa, Kansas, Massachusetts, Michigan, Minnesota, Missouri, Montana, Nebraska, New Hampshire, North Dakota, Ohio, Oklahoma, Oregon, Pennsylvania, South Dakota, Utah, West Virginia, Wisconsin, Washington, the provinces of New Brunswick and Ontario, and in Japan. If further evidence were desired, it would be furnished by the statistics for the current college year; for the students in attendance represent thirty-three states and territories of the American Union, and five foreign countries. So they come and go, and as they go each of them, it is hoped and believed, carries with him respect for law and order, and gives important aid in distributing the blessings of good government throughout the globe.

THOMAS M. COOLEY.

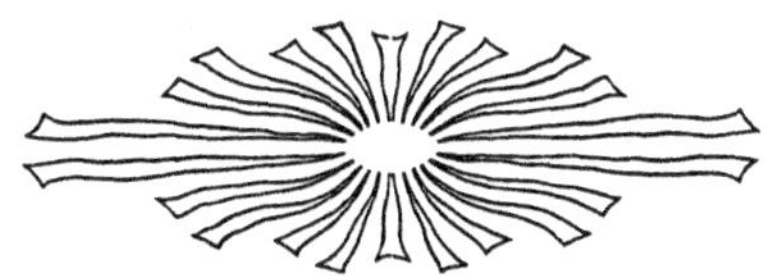

THE LAW BUILDING.

Judge Thomas McIntyre Cooley.

ATTENTION has often been called to the singular good fortune of our Law School in securing for its first Faculty three so eminent and successful teachers as Professors Campbell, Walker, and Cooley. It was equally fortunate in retaining them so many years. Judge Cooley, in his article in this publication, has dwelt somewhat on the services of his colleagues. This paper is intended to furnish some facts concerning his life and services, which for obvious reasons he could not be expected to present.

Thomas M. Cooley was by a year the junior of James V. Campbell. He was born in Attica, N. Y.. in 1824. While struggling against many adversities, he obtained his education at school and his professional preparation. He came to Michigan in 1843, and was admitted to the bar in Adrian in 1846. In 1857 he was selected to compile the General Statutes of Michigan, and in 1858 was appointed reporter of the Supreme Court. On his appointment to the professorship in the Law School, he removed to Ann Arbor. In 1864 he took his seat on the Supreme Bench, and retained it until 1885. When the Inter-State Commerce Commission was organized, he accepted, at the urgent solicitation of President Cleveland, the chairmanship of the Commission, which he retained until ill health compelled him to resign the post in 1891. He resigned the Jay Professorship of Law in 1884, but has almost every year given a few special lectures in the department.

He also took the chair of History and Constitutional Law, in the Literary Department, in 1885, and gave most valuable courses of lectures. He remained in this post until January 1, 1887. He has consented, at the urgent request of the Regents, to allow his name to stand on the Faculty list of the University Calendar, with the understanding that he should give an occasional lecture when the state of his health would permit. The lecture room is always crowded when it is known that he is to speak on any legal or historical topic.

As a lecturer on law, he was noted for the sharpness of his analysis, for the clearness with which he stated principles, for the legal learning with which he illustrated and expounded his statements, and for the breadth and soundness of his generalizations. He did not write his lectures. He spoke from brief notes slowly, and with such lucidity and precision of language that the students easily grasped and held his thoughts.

The fame which during the years of his connection with the Law School he was winning as a judge, and as an author of law treatises, was constantly bringing great honor to the school, and inspiring his students with the deepest respect for him and with pride in his achievements. As Dean and the only resident professor, he was brought into close personal contact with the students. He was ever accessible to them, his relations to them were most informal and friendly, they consulted him with the utmost freedom, and they always left the school with a mingled feeling towards him of gratitude and reverence. His untiring industry furnished a most stimulating example to them. His simple, but pure and noble, character left its impress on every student who was capable of being inspired by purity and nobility. The elevating influence which he exerted upon the personal and professional life of thousands of students who were under his care cannot be measured.

The records of the Law Department show that Judge Cooley's first lecture was given October 6, 1859. It was on the Origin of Title to Real Estate in America. His first lecture on constitutional law was delivered on October 4, 1860. It was entitled Constitutional Government. His subjects during his connection with the department were as follows: 1. Real Estate and Title Thereto, from 1859 to 1886, excepting the two years 1881–83; 2. Uses and Trusts, for the same time; 3. Constitutional Law, from 1860 to 1885; 4. Taxation, for the same period; 5. Domestic Relations, until 1883; 6. Wills and the Administration of Estates of Deceased Persons, until 1882; 7. Partnership, for fifteen years. After ceasing to lecture regularly in the department, he gave a course on Rights, Moral and Legal, and a course on The Inter-State Commerce Law. The records show that he frequently delivered to the students special lectures on subjects not called for in the regular course.

It seems proper to give here a list of the works which he has produced, most of them in connection with his work as law professor. Perhaps his Constitutional Limitations, which first appeared in 1868, is the work by which he is and will be most widely known. It has given him the reputation of one of the highest authorities on constitutional law wherever that subject is studied. In 1870 appeared his edition of Blackstone, in 1874 his edition of Story's Commentaries, in 1876 his Taxation, in 1879 his work on Torts, and in 1880 his Manual of Constitutional Law. In 1885 his History of Michigan was published, in the American Commonwealth Series.

Judge Cooley has been a frequent contributor to reviews upon important legal and governmental questions. He has also been called often to give addresses upon questions of law and history on important public occasions. The following is a fuller list of titles of such articles and addresses than has before been published, though it is not complete:

Some Checks and Balances in Government. International Review, May and June, 1876.

Limits to State Control of Private Business. Princeton Review, March, 1878.

Changes in the Balance of Governmental Powers. Address to the law students of the University of Michigan, 1878.

The Surrender of Fugitives from Justice. Princeton Review, January, 1879.

The Recording Laws of the United States, Their Inadequacy and Their Danger. Address before the American Bar Association, 1881.

Presidential Inability. North American Review, November, 1881.

State Regulation of Corporate Profits. North American Review, September, 1883.

The Abnegation of Self Government. Princeton Review, November, 1883.

Law as an Educating Force. Address at the Law Commencement, University of Michigan, 1884.

Codification. American Law Review, May and June 1886.

Arbitration in Labor Disputes. The Forum, June 1886.

The Influence of Habits of Thought upon Our Institutions. Address before the South Carolina Bar Association, 1886. (Rewritten and read in Ann Arbor, November 13, 1893.)

The Acquisition of Louisiana. Address before the Indiana Historical Society, 1887.

The Uncertainty of the Law. Address before the Georgia Bar Association, 1887.

On the Promulgation of the Constitution of Japan. Address at Johns Hopkins University, 1889.

Comparative Merits of Written and Prescriptive Constitutions. Address before the New York Bar Association, 1889. Also in Harvard Law Review, March, 1889.

The Place of the Federal Supreme Court in the American

Constitutional System. Address before the Political Science Association of the University of Michigan, 1889.

Federal Taxation of Lotteries. Atlantic Monthly, April, 1892.

Methods of Appointing Presidential Electors. Michigan Law Journal, February, 1892.

Sovereignty in the United States. Michigan Law Journal, April, 1892.

State Bank Issues in Michigan. Publications of the Michigan Political Science Association, No. 1, May, 1893.

Federal Taxation of State Bank Issues. Idem.

The Power to Amend the Federal Constitution. Michigan Law Journal, April, 1893.

Grave Obstacles to Hawaiian Annexation. The Forum, June, 1893.

The Administration of Justice in the United States in Civil Cases. Address before the World's Fair Auxiliary. Also in Michigan Law Journal, September, 1893.

Independence of the Legislative Department of Government. Argument before the Supreme Court of Michigan, 1893.

*Liability of Public Officers to Private Actions for Neglect of Duty. Southern Law Review, 1877.

The Semi-Centennial of Michigan. Address delivered at the celebration of the State Semi-Centennial, 1886.

What the Law Can Do for the Health of the People. Address at a State Sanitary Convention.

The Cases in Which the Master is Liable for Injuries. Southern Law Review, 1876.

The Judicial Functions of Surveyors, 1852.

What Shall be Done With Our Ex-Presidents? Contribution to a Symposium. The Century, Dec. 1885.

Judge Cooley's work on the Inter-State Commerce Commission was performed after he left his chair in the Law Department. He brought to it the best powers of his ripest years. I have heard one of his colleagues on the Commission

* This paper opens with a sentence which has now become somewhat famous, "a public office is a public trust." Several persons have been credited with the first utterance of it. There seems no reason to doubt that Judge Cooley is the original author of the expression.

say that Judge Cooley did for the body of inter-state commerce law what Marshall did for the Constitution, in determining its scope and meaning. In the conscientious discharge of his duties he probably overtasked his constitution, to whose powers of endurance, for thirty years, there had seemed to be no limit. But in these late years of tedious illness, which have set a limit to his physical activity, though not to his mental, his interest in the fortunes of the Law School and the University, to whose service he has devoted so much of his life, has remained unabated. Long may he be spared to rejoice in its prosperity, and to delight its students and its professors, as he is pleased to do from time to time, by appearing upon the rostrum where he lectured to twenty-five successive classes.

JAMES B. ANGELL.

Write a Poem for To Wit:

WRITE a poem for "To Wit:"
Hurry up the moments flit,
Never mind what comes of it,
Write a poem for "To Wit:"

Make it either short or long,
Make the metre right or wrong,
Let the thought be weak or strong,
Write a jolly college song.

Write a lawyer's poor complaint,
Tell of night winds murmuring faint,
Sing of mortals; sing of saint;
Use words commonplace or quaint—

But—write a poem for "To Wit:"
Never mind what comes of it;
Hurry up the moments flit,
Write a poem for "To Wit:"

WALTER HERMANN KIRK.

CHRISTIAN H. BUHL.

Christian H. Buhl.

THE University of Michigan has a law library of about 11,000 volumes. This is much larger than can be found in many educational institutions and for this we are chiefly indebted to Christian H. Buhl, of Detroit, who has recently died leaving to the University a bequest of $10,000, to be expended in completing the library already given us. This money judiciously applied will furnish the department with one of the best law libraries connected with any American university.

The Department of Law in this University was established in 1859. A most excellent Faculty was selected, but there were no books to work with. The Regents made some delicate appropriations which met the emergency. A private donation, however, became the nucleus of what we now possess. In 1866 Richard Fletcher, of Boston, Mass., once a Judge of the Supreme Court of that state, gave his private library to our Law Department. His portrait hangs on the walls of the lecture room, reminding us of his disinterested benevolence. Judge Fletcher was closely related by marriage to Charles I. Walker, then a member of our Law Faculty. He was born at Cavendish, Vt., January 8, 1788, and died at Boston January 21, 1869. He graduated in law at Dartmouth, studied with Daniel Webster, and in 1836 defeated Charles Sumner, in a congressional election. He was a member of the Supreme Court of Massachusetts from 1848 to 1853, and reached a very high standard as a lawyer and a jurist. The New England colleges showered their honors upon him. The degree of LL. D. was conferred by Brown, Dartmouth and Harvard. Through careful business management he became very wealthy, and used his wealth to advance education. During his life he gave over $100,000 to Dartmouth College. His donation to us, although comparatively small, has always been kindly remembered.

The records of the University contain a copy of his letter, sent in reply to an acknowledgment of his gift. The letter was written from Boston on July 16, 1866. Among other things, he said: "It affords me pleasure to know that the books, which I collected in the course of a long professional life, will not be scattered, but will remain together for the use of the students in the Law Department of the great University of the Northwest. The Board of Regents, in giving my name to a professorship of law, have conferred an honor on me which I desire most gratefully to acknowledge. The University of Michigan must surely be regarded with admiration by all who are acquainted with its history and its present condition, and have a just apprehension of its greatness and usefulness in the future." Over twenty-five years have passed since this letter was written. We have his library carefully preserved and believe that his expectations have been realized.

On the opposite page of the record, from which we have quoted, appear some statistics regarding the attendance at the University in 1866, which may interest us, even though they do not pertain to the subject of this article.

The number of students was as follows:

Department of Science, Literature and the Arts......	353
Department of Medicine and Surgery................	467
Department of Law.............................	385

These figures suggest many things that we havn't the time to speak of. The Literary Department was then the weakest in numbers and was little more than a scientific school. Great changes have taken place. Under President Angell's administration the professional departments have been encouraged and have prospered, but the University has been steadily pushed along the lines of liberal culture. This has added value to every degree conferred.

In 1885 President Angell received from Christian H. Buhl a brief note containing these words: "I have a law library of about four thousand volumes, principally reports, which I propose to give to the University if it will be of use. Should it be thought best to accept these books, delivery can be made at once." It is hardly necessary to say that the University authorities and students highly appreciated this very liberal gift. In the printed record of the proceedings of the Board of Regents is found the correspondence between Mr. Buhl, the President of the University, the Law Faculty and the students of the Law Department. The students resolved to take steps to secure a portrait of Mr. Buhl "to be placed in the lecture room as a permanent memento of his munificence." The portrait was afterwards presented by Mr. Buhl and now hangs on the east wall of the lecture room.

In President Angell's letter accepting the gift our needs at that time, were stated. He wrote: "To show you that it will be of great use to us, I may say that it will fill many sad gaps in our law library. How serious these gaps are I almost hesitate to say. But the truth is that although we have law students from all over the Union, there are thirty states and territories which are absolutely unrepresented by a single volume of reports. * * We have only 4,400 volumes in all."

Mr. Buhl had collected this library for the benefit of the citizens of Detroit. He was not a lawyer, but some of the leading members of the Detroit bar were his personal friends and daily associates. Their needs were made known to him. Actuated by that generous public spirit, which guided him throughout his life, he caused to be carefully selected a complete library of English and American text-books and reports. This collection became his pet. He enjoyed seeing it grow. Its care was his diversion.

In 1884 certain changes were made in Detroit which deprived the Buhl library of its original field of usefulness. Mr. Buhl was troubled to know what to do with it. It was valued at $15,000, although much more had been spent in collecting it. He was besieged by book agents who were anxious to sell it for him. Many publishing houses offered to purchase it. For six months he considered the subject and finally determined that it should not be sold. He did not relish the idea of witnessing the breaking up of what he had taken so much pains in collecting. To one of his friends he said: "I will place that library where it will be forever preserved. I will give it to the University of Michigan." A happy thought. He devoted his library to the cause of legal education and thus thousands of young men have been assisted through his generosity.

Mr. Buhl was born in Butler County, Pennsylvania, on May 9, 1812. His parents came from Saxony and he was one of a family of eleven children. His father was a merchant and a farmer of small means, with large expenses. He could not give his children the advantages of a liberal education. He gave his boys a common school education and a trade. The subject of this sketch learned the trade of hatter, and, at the age of twenty-one, came West to cut his way in the wilderness, He reached Detroit in 1833, an ambitious but wholly inexperienced lad.

The City of the Straits was then a small town of about 2,500 inhabitants. It was the only incorporated town in the Territory. There were a few stores, many small houses, and a large fort to protect the inhabitants against the Indians. There was nothing inviting except the remnants of the Black Hawk War and the fear of Asiatic cholera, which the year before had nearly depopulated the town.

Many of the most eminent men in the history of Michigan came into the State about this time. In the same year Zachariah Chandler settled in Detroit, and Alpheus Felch hung out his shingle in Monroe. James V. Campbell, Elon Farnsworth, known as Chancellor Farnsworth, Jacob S. Farrand and Alexander Frazer had reached Detroit only a few years before Mr. Buhl, and within the next three years Theodore H. Hinchman, James F. Joy, Thomas McGraw, Theodore Romeyn and Henry P. Baldwin came to the growing town to make for themselves and the good of society. All now know how well they succeeded. The hamlet in the woods has become a metropolis, and the wild territory a prosperous and growing State. The people of Michigan will never fully realize how much they owe to that phalanx of young men who came here in the early thirties. Christian H. Buhl cast his lot with them and quietly carried more than his share of the burdens.

Mr. Buhl was a far-seeing man. He was not discouraged by present difficulties. The American Fur Company, with its trading posts throughout the Northwest, attracted his attention. He formed a partnership with his brother, Frederick Buhl, under the firm name of F. & C. H. Buhl. They opened a hat and cap store at Detroit, then engaged in the fur business, and soon became the largest dealers in furs in the West. Their business extended over Michigan, Ohio, Indiana, Illinois, Wisconsin and Upper Canada.

In 1853 Mr. Buhl and his brother dissolved partnership, and soon thereafter he engaged in the hardware and iron business with Charles Ducharme, under the firm name of Buhl & Ducharme. This became his life work, and he continued it until his death. He accumulated a large fortune. In 1873 Mr. Ducharme died. The eldest son, Theodore D. Buhl, was admitted to the firm. For over twenty years the father and his two sons carried on a very extensive business, the magnitude of which we are not permitted to state. To say nothing of their large property interests in Detroit, we may say that, at Mr. Buhl's death, they owned and operated, in connection with their Detroit business, the Western Iron Company's works, located at Sharon, Pennsylvania, and valued at over $1,000,000. These works give employment to 1,000 men.

During his life Mr. Buhl was interested in many important business enterprises. At one time he owned a controlling interest in the Detroit Locomotive Works. He was for many years the acting president of the Second National Bank of Detroit. He was largely responsible for the building of two lines of railroad in the State: the Detroit, Hillsdale & Indiana, and the Detroit, Eel River & Illinois. For a time he was president of both roads. In politics he was a Republican, but not a partisan. He held but one political office, that of Mayor of the City of Detroit for the years of 1860 and 1861. He was a thorough Christian gentleman and a regular attendant of the Presbyterian church, to which he made large contributions.

In 1843 he was married to Miss Caroline D. Long, of

Utica, New York. She came west to carry her half up the hill. At once Mr. Buhl's home was full of peace and comfort, a place of refuge from the exhausting activities of the business world. No one enjoyed it more than he. The happiness of his home was his greatest pleasure. He was a thoroughly domestic man. Four children, two sons and two daughters survive him. His sons continue in the business of their father, who has left them not only a large fortune, but that which is far more valuable the impress of his traits of character, and a vast experience in correct business methods.

In many respects Mr. Buhl was a most remarkable man. He was always candid and self possessed. During his active business career of over sixty years in the City of Detroit, he was frequently engaged in transactions involving many millions. The magnitude of an undertaking, the prospect of success or the danger of failure never unbalanced his judgment. He wasted no time or strength in imagining good or evil. His habits of living were becoming to his station in life, but were very simple and pure. He suffered no indulgence that could in any way impair his constitution or weaken his power for good in society. He was a self-made man. At the threshold of life he learned to preserve every physical, intellectual and moral force in him. Having learned this lesson he never forgot it.

His business habits were very severe. Nothing could divert him from what he had previously agreed to do. He was not a man of apologies. He looked doubtingly on any excuse offered for the breach of a business engagement. The man who committed the breach lost favor and regained it with difficulty. Mr. Buhl was charitable and forgiving, but he measured men by the promptness and thoroughness with which they fulfilled the most trivial obligations. Up to within a few weeks before his death he was at his office regularly at hours which all understood. Every one knew when and where to find Christian H. Buhl. It is said that one could tell to a minute when his footsteps would be heard on the stairway leading to his office. He was over eighty years old when he died. This inflexible rule of conduct had governed him for more than sixty years. He could not depart from it because it had become a part of himself. To this trait of character may be largely attributed his ability to manage successfully so many and so varied business interests.

Some men excuse a mis-statement or a false coloring of facts on the ground that it was made by an interested party. The world is full of casuistry. Mr. Buhl did not indulge in it. He was a man of startling mental veracity. Our Professor Kirchner, who was for many years his counsellor, relates an incident. Condemnation proceedings were pending against Mr. Buhl. At the hearing, the question in dispute was the value of the lands to be taken. The greater the value of the lands the greater the damage to be assessed in favor of Mr. Buhl. He was financially interested in having them highly appraised. Many influential men, thoroughly familiar with the value of real estate, took the stand and gave their testimony in his behalf. He was called as a witness and, to the surprise of all present, gave a valuation far below the estimates of many who had appeared for him. This was a striking and unusual performance, but it clearly illustrated Mr. Buhl's character. He was genuine in everything that he did or said. Unfortunately he said very little. His conscience controlled him and did not forsake him when he entered the witness box. We see now why the people of Detroit were continually thrusting upon him positions of responsibility, where large financial interests were involved.

An active business life, long continued, sometimes shrivels a man's heart. Occasionally, however, a man appears who is great enough to amass a fortune and at the same time develop a benevolent spirit. Mr. Buhl was a quiet but continuous and methodical giver. During his life he gave away annually thousands of dollars to the poor and to various eleemosynary, religious and educational institutions. Most of the numerous legatees named in his will, have been for many years the objects of his bounty. It is said that, on the first of January of each year, he carefully estimated how much of his income could be given to humanity, then named the donees and the portion which each should receive. This contract with himself he faithfully fulfilled. The act was not hearalded before the public. It was a part of his private life. He did not give that his giving might be known. In this respect he was decidedly individual, but every man will be slow to criticize. Modesty is a becoming virtue, which Mr. Buhl possessed in a very high degree.

After Mr. Buhl's death we find that his watchful eye has been upon us, ever since his first munificient gift. He gives by his will $10,000 to the Law Library of our University. It is fair to say that this bequest was made without the solicitation or knowledge of any person connected, directly or indirectly, with the University. Mr. Buhl acted for himself, guided by his own generous impulse. In making the bequest he has, unconsciously perhaps, built for himself a monument of books. Thousands of students will consult them for years and years to come, and then, following his example, may go West to build another state like Michigan, and would that they could fill it with men like Christian H. Buhl. Certain it is that his long, severe but beautiful life will be to them a more valuable lesson that can be drawn from books.

JEROME C. KNOWLTON.

A Postscript.

THE attorney is the only representative, in this age of the Knights-errant of old, that pure-minded, valiant and chivalric body of men who went forth into the world seeking out wrongs that they might right them, aiding the weak against the mighty, setting the captive free, slaying dragons. Like those old knights you have had to endure vigils, watchings, discipline that you may be able, when the time comes to prove your right to be called a Knight, an Attorney. And now, as you are about to ride forth, I am asked to give you a word of counsel.

Well, bear in mind Don Quixote and the wind mills, and avoid all such encounters by taking counsel with common sense and the law, those gentle and wise Sancho Panzas. If you find yourself at any time, as you often may, between the devil and the deep sea, turn your back to the sea and face the devil.

It is not an easy task to give advice that is of any value, that will be of any real advantage and assistance. As a rule advice is not a savory dish; if it is not actually flavored with bitter herbs it is distressingly insipid, made up of goody platitudes, that have been warmed over and over again until the mixture has a hash-like appearance and a bread-pudding flavor. During the last two years you of the senior class have been regaled from time to time with some of these delectable dishes. The ingredients were good and originally wholesome;

if found harmful it is the fault of the cook. For instance, we have served up that substantial joint, *piece de resistance*, knowledge of the law, and you have been seriously and solemnly advised not to shun and avoid altogether a slight acquaintance, at least, with the law. This is most admirable advice, and you have listened to it with commendable attention.

No serious trouble has resulted, apparently. Of course the advice is an heir loom in the profession. It is not the less valuable on that account. The returning seasons are old as creation, but none chide the fresh breeze of spring because it opened the roses for Adam in his youth and has annually romped around the earth since.

You have been advised also to acquire a knowledge of human nature, that your knowledge of the law may be administered in a manner that shall be safe for you and dangerous to your adversary only. The man who would teach a dog some trick must first of all master the dog's view of the matter. You cannot hope to induce a twenty-four-legged jury to turn hand-springs and stand on its head unwittingly without the "sesame" that opens the doors to the secret chambers of the human heart.

The source of all knowledge of others is knowledge of yourself. Whether such self knowledge is a safe and sure guide depends upon whether as a man you are true or false. The rascal can study the motives of an honest man and acquire that same kind and degree of information which the scientific observer obtains in regard to the phenomena of nature. But the gift to think the thoughts of the Almighty is inspiration, and knowledge of the motives of the pure and upright is given to the pure and upright only. Since you must judge others yourself, your self knowledge should be something worth by knowing and not altogether worthless and deceptive, for there is no deception so deceptive and misleading as self deception. It is therefore of the utmost importance to the lawyer, from the standpoint of knowledge and power, simply, that he should be honest, generous, unselfish, pure minded, a lover of justice and equity, a good hater of evil, of wrong and oppression, and that all high and lofty motives should well up from his heart, permeate his whole being and characterize and beautify his whole life and not be assumed and put on, like my lady's powder and rouge, for an occasion. Those virtues are the common inheritance of mankind. It is true that some have them in a very rudimentary state, and in others they have been smothered or else have been pruned and trained into such a semblance of vice as would deceive St. Peter himself. Few persons may possess all of them in sweet perfection. Still they are found in every jury box, and the lawyer who seeks a verdict must not overlook them, much less scorn and defy them. It is always safe to assume, if you are honest and fearless, that the reasons and arguments which have led you to believe that your client ought to have a verdict will compel the jury to give you that verdict.

Next to honesty, legal learning and knowledge of human nature, ranks the virtue of modesty. All lawyers are modest, but some possess this virtue to a greater extent than others. By modesty we do not mean diffidence. Diffidence in a lawyer is not a virtue. Diffidence in him is a vice, since it implies want of confidence in the justness of his cause, or in his own ability, and leads the observer to doubt also. We mean modesty of deportment, of conduct and bearing in the trial of a cause.

Good taste and the art of the orator demand that the attorney shall not attract to himself the attention of either the court or jury. He is a mere advocate. His purpose from first to last should be to have his cause absorb the entire attention of both court and jury. Every argument advanced, every gesture made, every intonation of the voice should have that object solely in view. A period, however beautiful, an illustration, however apt, which for a moment diverts the attention of the jury from your cause to yourself, is a sad failure. Few jurymen can think of two things at the same time, and if their thoughts are upon you, your client is forgotten. Cultivate the art of compelling them to remember your client and to forget yourself. There is no danger of your being forgotten altogether. You will be remembered after the verdict.

Clients are necessary to success. You cannot win a verdict without having first won a client. There is an excellent recipe for cooking a hare, the first direction being, catch a hare. Now a client is a person who has legal work to do and wants it done. He employs a lawyer, not for sweet charity's sake, nor out of love for the profession, nor to give some deserving young man a start. His motives are much nearer the earth. He is buying something he wants, and he never intends to pay more than the article is worth. He may, of course, for the world is full of uncertainty. He is often guided in his choice of an attorney by faith, and the size of the retainer is the measure of his faith, "the substance of things hoped for, the evidence of things not seen." Do not anticipate a large retainer from your first client, except as a charge to profit and loss. It is still permissable to marry for love and to take a first client for the hope of glory. Now how are you to inspire some poor rich man with faith in your learning and ability? It is often a difficult task, but the difficulties must add zeal merely to the undertaking. Your knowledge of the law will not aid you materially, for your first client will not be a lawyer, and he will be unable to judge of your legal attainments. He will infer your knowledge, or want of knowledge, from your grasp of some subject with which he is familiar and in which he takes a special interest. You must not, therefore, talk your own shop, but the other fellow's. Talking shop may not be in good form, but it is sure delight the owner of the shop and to impress him with the to worth of the man who appreciates that particular shop and its appurtenances. Tristam Shandy has observed that every man has his hobby horse, and Shandy could tell the truth when not inspired. A lawyer should not be ignorant of hobby horses. Not that you may have one of your own, but that you may be considerate of your neighbors. If you desire to impress a good man with your learning, good sense and wisdom, ride his hobby horse. Ride him like a true horseman, well and furiously, and you will capture his heart and—win a client. Politicians go about the country kissing babies. That, too, is permissable when the age and sex of the baby are suitable. But if you may choose between the baby and the hobby horse, take the hobby horse. A mother's love for her child is beautiful and enduring, but a strong man's admiration and affection for his hobby horse is steadfast and touching. Now if you should observe that this is not an exalted view of human nature, I should reply that your observation was irrelevant, immaterial and inadmissable. The question just now is, how to catch a client.

Much more could be added to this postscript, but I am certain it is unnecessary since you remember, of course, all the good and sensible advice that has been given during the past two years by the one and the other of your teachers.

"Watchman, what of the night?" If you are honest and faithful, add continually to your knowledge of the law, acquire a profound knowledge of human nature, and are willing and able to fast occasionally for the first few years, you are reasonably certain of obtaining ultimately the success you may merit. "The mills of the gods grind slow, but they grind exceeding small." Do not fear or shun those mills. Have all your harvests ground there.

BRADLEY M. THOMPSON.

INTERIOR VIEW OF THE PRACTICE COURT.

The Practice Court.

LOOKED at from different standpoints, the law may be said to be both a science and an art. It is certainly one of the most practical of sciences. History shows that it had its origin in the practical solution of primitive controversies, and it is along practical lines that its development has been had. It was practical before it was theoretical, and the same rule still prevails. Law exists, not for its own sake, but as a means to an end, namely, the creation and protection of human rights. The final test of every legal principle is not its abstract or theoretical correctness but its capacity for practical application to the affairs of men. The final test of every position is its capacity to be maintained by the actual application of the practical rules of the forum. Practice, therefore, occupies a prominent part, not only in the development and application of the law, but also in the work and duties of the lawyer.

It has often been urged as the chief, if not the only objection to instruction in law schools that their training was, and of necessity must be, purely theoretical and not practical in its character. As to the theoretical side, it has long been conceded that the law school furnished an opportunity to become grounded in legal principles which were furnished no where else; but as to the practical side, it has been insisted that only the law office and the court room could furnish the necessary training. To admit this, and it long seemed that it must be admitted, was to acknowledge that the law school did but half of its professed work, namely, the training of lawyers. To send the student out equipped only with a mass of rules and principles which he knew not how to apply—to supply him with tools which he knew not how to use—was only to send him out to become an easy prey for his brother lawyer, trained in the practical atmosphere of the law office and the courts. Many a young lawyer has gone out from the law schools well versed in legal principles, only to be nonplussed by the first practical difficulty.

To supply this need as far as possible the law schools have, for many years, adopted the moot court and encouraged the formation of club courts among the students. The difficulty with the former is that they give but little practical training, being chiefly occupied with the argument of pure questions of law, while in the latter, presided over and conducted by the students themselvcs, there is neither the incentive which comes with required work nor any certainty that their methods or conclusions are correct. There was obviously an imperative need for something better, and this need has led to the establishment, in the Law Department of the University, of the practice court. Experiment had convinced the Faculty that it could be done, and it was accordingly projected upon lines and to an extent not only never before attempted in the history of law schools, but declared elsewhere to be impracticable if not impossible. It is believed that it is not too much to say that experience has now demonstrated that it is both practicable and possible, and that it supplies the need which has so long been felt.

The practice court has become a part of the department. It has been generously equipped by the Board of Regents with the material facilities required. A commodious and convenient room has been fitted with all of the machinery of an actual court room; another room has been supplied for the office of the clerk, and it has been furnished with appropriate fittings and equipped with a full supply of the blanks and forms in common use in the several states; a clerk has been provided, paid by the University, whose time and services are at the command of the practitioners, and the various members of the Faculty sit daily as judges.

The work has been divided into two courses: First, a course of cases upon statements of facts, prepared and assigned by the Faculty, upon which causes are to be begun, issues of law framed, and arguments had upon the legal points involved as in actual practice. This course embraces not only the practice of the old moot courts, but, in addition, the actual commencement of the action and its prosecution to a judgment upon the issues of law involved. Second, a course of cases upon actual controversies arranged among the students by members of the Faculty, in which the students assigned as attorneys are to collect the evidence, determine the forum and form of action, sue out process and conduct the cause to its termination. These cases are usually tried by jury, and all of the practice of selecting a jury, examining and cross-examining witnesses, arguing questions of law to the court and of fact to the jury, substantially as in actual trials, is obtained. In this course, a jury trial will be found in progress upon substantially every day in the second semester. Each student is required to take part as attorney in at least one case in each course, besides performing duty as witness, juror, party and officer as required. The practice and procedure in each course are according to that prevailing in the student's own state.

The work devolved upon the Faculty has been very

great. Methods of procedure have required to be evolved, rules prepared, and all of the complicated machinery of the court and the clerk's office put in motion. The labor of preparing over seventy-five different statements of fact for the first course has been great, but not so great as that of arranging as many actual controversies for jury trials in the second course. The members of the class have entered into the work with the zest which ensures success. Never before has there been such a generous rivalry in work; such demands upon the library; such a spirit of inquiry and investigation in the air.

It is not pretended that this work can make trained lawyers in the larger sense, but there is here afforded an opportunity to learn the methods of actual practice, to test one's tools before commencing their life use, to "wear off the rough edges," to make one's "bad breaks" where they can be corrected and do no harm, and generally to acquire, with the guidance of friendly instructors and in an atmosphere of fraternal sympathy, much of that practical knowledge which comes only with hard knocks and often humiliating experience when first learned in actual practice.

It seems not too much to say that with the establishment of the practice court, the addition of the new course of lectures, the munificent gift for the library, which was already one of the largest and best equipped to be found in the law schools of this country, the recent enlargement of the building, and that *esprit de corps* and generous emulation which come from the association of a larger number of law students than are gathered together any where else upon this continent, the Law Department of the University of Michigan may be relied upon to continue and enlarge that career of usefulness which in the past has made it the leading law school of the land.

FLOYD R. MECHEM.

H.L.R.
Fraternities
in Order
of
Establishment.

The Legal Fraternity of Phi Delta Phi.

Founded at University of Michigan, 1869.

Chapter Roll.

Kent,	University of Michigan,	1869
Booth,	Union College of Law, Chicago,	1877
Story,	Columbia College,	1881
Cooley,	St. Louis Law School,	1882
Pomeroy,	University of California,	1884
Marshall,	Washington Law Schools,	1884
Webster,	Boston University,	1885
Hamilton,	Cincinnati Law School,	1886
Gibson,	University of Pennsylvania,	1886
Waite,	Yale University,	1887
Choate,	Harvard University,	1887
Field,	New York University,	1888
Conkling,	Cornell University,	1888
Tiedeman,	University of Missouri,	1890
Minor,	University of Virginia,	1890
Dillon,	University of Minnesota,	1890
Daniels,	Buffalo Law School,	1891
Chase,	Oregon Law School,	1891
Harlan,	University of Wisconsin,	1891
Swan,	Ohio State University,	1893
McClain,	University of Iowa,	1893

E. A. WRIGHT, PHILA.
797

Phi Delta Phi.

Kent Chapter Established 1869.

Fratres in Facultate.

Hon. Thomas McIntyre Cooley, LL. D., Α Δ Φ,
Prof. Jerome Cyril Knowlton, A. B., LL. B., Ζ Ψ,
Hon. Levi Thomas Griffin, A. M., Β Θ Π,
Prof. Otto Kirchner,
Prof. Bradley Martin Thompson, M. S., LL. B., ΔΚΕ,
Justice Henry B. Brown, LL. D.,
Judge John W. Champlin, LL. D.,
Prof. Floyd R. Mechem,
Elias F. Johnson, B. S., LL. M.,
Dr. William Gardiner Hammond, Cooley Chapter, A. M., Ph. D., Ψ Υ.
Hon. Melville Madison Bigelow, Webster Chapter, A. M., Ph. D.

Fratres in Urbe.

Judge Edward D. Kinne, A. B., Σ Φ,
Hon. Charles R. Whitman, A. B.,
Ora Elmer Butterfield, LL. B.,
Pomeroy Ladue, B. S., LL. B., Ζ Ψ,
Jonn R. Effinger, Ph. B., LL. B., Φ Κ Ψ.

Fratres in Universitate.

1894.

Alfred Franklin Bissell, Β Θ Π,
Henry Ernest Candler, B. S., Ζ Ψ.
Holbrook Gilson Cleaveland, A. B., Ψ Υ,
Walter Shepard Fulton,
William Rhodes Hervey, B. S., Κ Α,
John Stanley Hurd, A. B, Ψ Υ,
Franz Christian Kuhn, B. S.,
Samuel Medbury, Δ Κ Ε,
William Goodpaster Ramsay, A. B., Β Θ Π,
Hedley Vicars Richardson, Ph. B.,
Daniel Lindsay Russell, Δ Κ Ε,
James J. Sheridan,
John Grover Stone, Β Θ Π,
Luther Ogden Wadleigh, Ph. B., Δ Κ Ε,
Percy Wilson, A. B., Θ Δ Χ,
HARRY Fralick Worden, Α Δ Φ.

1895.

Elmer Louis Allor, B. S,
Ira Charles Belden, Ph. B., Φ Κ Ψ,
Harry Conant Bulkley, A. B., Δ Κ Ε,
John Sidney Burnet,
Henry Howard Cushing, Δ Κ Ε,
Robert Winfield Dunn, Β Θ Π,
Harry Irving Dunton, Χ Ψ,
Allan Pegram Gilmour, A. B.,
Charles Belknap Henderson, Ph. B., Φ Κ Ψ,
Rufus Gillett Lathrop, A. B., Δ Κ Ε,
Charles Sumner McDowell, Β Θ Π,
Edgar Martin Morsman, Ph. B., Φ Κ Ψ,
Victor John Obenauer, Ph. B., B. S., Π Α Φ,
Edward Sidney Rogers.

Fraternity of Kappa Sigma.

Founded at University of Bologna, Italy, 1395. Established in America at University of Virginia, 1867.

Chapter Roll.

GAMMA,	State University of Louisiana.
DELTA,	Davidson College.
EPSILON,	Centenary College.
ZETA,	University of Virginia.
ETA,	Randolph-Macon College, Va.
THETA,	Cumberland University.
IOTA,	Southwestern University.
KAPPA,	Vanderbilt University.
LAMBDA,	University of Tennessee.
MU,	Washington and Lee University.
NU,	William and Mary College.
XI,	University of Arkansas.
OMICRON,	Emory and Henry College.
PI,	Swarthmore College.
RHO,	North Georgia College.
SIGMA,	Tulane University.
TAU,	University of Texas.
UPSILON,	Hampden-Sidney College.
PHI,	Southwestern Presbyterian Univ.
CHI,	Purdue University.
PSI,	Maine State College.
OMEGA,	University of the South.
CHI-OMEGA,	University of South Carolina.
ALPHA-ALPHA,	Johns Hopkins University.
ALPHA-BETA,	Mercer University.
ALPHA-GAMMA,	University of Illinois.
ALPHA-DELTA,	Pennsylvania State College.
ALPHA-EPSILON,	University of Pennsylvania.
ALPHA-ZETA,	University of Michigan.
ALPHA-ETA,	Columbian University.
ALPHA-THETA,	Southwestern Baptist University.
ALPHA-IOTA,	U. S. Grant University.
ALPHA-KAPPA,	Cornell University.
ALPHA-LAMBDA,	University of Vermont.
ETA-PRIME,	Trinity College.
ALPHA-MU,	University of North Carolina.
ALPHA-NU,	Wofford College.

Alumni Associations.

ALPHA ALUMNI,	Yazoo City, Mississippi.
PHILADELPHIA ALUMNI CLUB,	Philadelphia, Pennsylvania.
PITTSBURG ALUMNI CLUB,	Pittsburg, Pennsylvania.
NEW ORLEANS ALUMNI CLUB,	New Orleans.
GALVESTON ALUMNI CLUB,	Galveston, Texas.
WASHINGTON ALUMNI CLUB,	Washington, D. C.

ΚΣ
BONONIA
ΣΟΦΙΑ
ΧΡΗΜΑΤΑ
και
ΔΥΝΑΜΙΣ
ΚΑΡΤΕΡΙΑ
ΑΛΗΘΕΙΑ
ΔΙΚΗ
ΠΙΣΤΟΤΗΣ
SEMPER

Dreka. Phila.

Kappa Sigma.

Alpha Zeta Chapter, Established 1892.

Literary Department.

1897.

Ernest Elwood Ford, LL. B.,

Medical Department.

1897.

Rolla Joseph Baldwin, B. S. Tau.

Law Department.

1894.

Joseph Edmund Barrell,
George Washington Fuller,
John Ward Powers,
Fred Wilbur Smith,
Julius Curtis Travis,
Charles Arza Denison, B. L.,
Allen Gurracy Mills, B. S.,
Guy Leonidas Reed,
McKenzie Robertson Todd,
Charles Eugene Ward.

1895.

Harry Boardman Anderson,
Percy Beaugrand Champagne,
Franklin Lewis Edinborough,
LeRoy Palmer,
Warren Wesley Travis,
Walter Scott Carr, Α Γ, Alpha Gamma,
Willis Sherman Clark,
Charles Lemuel DeVault,
Lindley Grant Long,
Glen Beal Roseberry,
Henry Martin Zimmerman.

Legal Fraternity of Delta Chi.

Founded at Cornell University, 1890.

Chapter Roll.

Cornell University.

University of the City of New York.

Union College.

University of Michigan.

University of Minnesota.

Dickinson College.

Northwestern University.

Dreka. Phila.

Delta Chi.

Michigan Chapter, Established 1892.

Fratres Honorarii.

Judge William G. Ewing,
Judge Samuel Maxwell,
Hon. Jonathan P. Dollivar, A. B.,
Hon. Roger Q. Mills,
Hon. Robert T. Lincoln,
Prof. Marshall D. Ewell, LL D.,
Prof. Herman V. Ames, Ph. D.,
Prof. John B. Clayberg, LL. B.,
Judge Victor A. Elliott,
James L. High.

Fratres in Universitate.

1894.

Harry Howard Patterson, B. S.,
Charles Arthur Park, A. M., Φ Δ Θ,
Robert Clowry Chapman,
Sherman Clark Spitzer, B. L.,
Charles Orlando Duncan,
Charles Whitney Chapman,
Milton Edward Blake,
Willis Victor Elliott,
Robert Bruce Mitchell.

1895.

Harry Hemphill Parsons, A. B.,
Thomas Scott Hayden, Jr.,
Arthur Calvin Bartels,
Llewellyn Barton Case,
Frank Warren Ballinger,
Edward Horsky, A. B.,
T. Myron Westover,
Philo G. Burnham, B. S.,
Walter Millard Ellett, Ph. B.,
Fred H. Gaston, B. S.,
Schuyler Colfax Hubbell,
Thornton Dixon.

Class Song.

SLOWLY now the portals swing,
Resounding with the songs we sing,
For happy are we,
Beyond them to see,
The broad and distant fertile fields,
Wherein we yearn
To toil and earn,
The valued fruits which culture yields.

CHORUS:
Away! Away!
Ambition bids us no delay—
Success to win,
Our works begin,
And we must to them haste away!

Though we our ways may often lose—
Though we diverging paths may choose,
Across the plain,
'Mid trials and pain,
Abreast its fortunes pressing on,
Yet mem'ries dear,
Of friends known here,
Our hearts will tune to friendship's song.

CHORUS:

WALTER HERMANN KIRK.

History of the Class of Ninety=Four.

IT IS customary among those associated in the noble aim of acquiring academic and professional degrees to adopt some plan of perpetuating their loyalty to the cause they have espoused. The numbers who have gone before can fully attest the value of such efforts in effectually increasing the affinity of students for their labors in any department. There should be few so covetous of the laurels they have won, or so sensitive to just reproof for inadvertence, that they would not gladly enrich the welfare of posterity with the valuable contribution of a varied experience. This becomes the more important as successive classes strive with jealous zeal to merit favorable recognition from a worthy Alma Mater.

In the clear autumnal days of '92, nearly three hundred members, with unpolished ability and crude opinions, assembled as the class of '94. They hailed from every quarter of the country, and many from without its confines. The conservatism of the East, the activity of the North, the valor of the South, and the progressiveness of the West joined hands upon equal terms in the race for professional proficiency. The man of means, the victim of pinching poverty, and the pampered sons of plenty mingled alike with the sturdy progeny of the rural district in that inexhaustible resource of brain supply. And these conditions constitute one of the great advantages in the history of this class. To be brought in close communion with divergent views and individual peculiarities in a common pursuit instills a full and appreciative realization of our identity of purpose and unity of interest. Provincialism fades away and our separation, by the lines of state boundaries, exists only in contemplation of law.

A class numerically large and mentally powerful, with a wholesome regard for honest differences, breeds a spirit of emulation and ambition that can be brought into existence in no other way. Its brings gratification to perceptors and valuable results to students that cannot be acquired in local or isolated institutions. Students of schools of narrow scope and character learn in a legal way that jurisdictions are foreign, and the same feeling and distinction is unconsciously absorbed socially. Learning must have breadth as well as depth before it bears the substantial fruit of practical application. Anything powerful is powerful for good or for evil accordingly as it is directed, and it has sometimes been hinted that the verbal contentions of the champions of antagonistic legal principles have overleaped the bounds of propriety to the disturbance of the dignity and reserve of peaceful neighbors. It is, however, the fortunate task of the present chronicler to state that this year has witnessed a material innovation in this respect. Perhaps no class has spent more time and energy in imbibing copious draughts of learning from the reservoirs of legal erudition. That there should be occasional reactions of an explosive character is only in keeping with the spirit of the work consigned to those who constitute the seismic vertical of campus ability. The irregular outbursts of genius and the sparkling gems of wit have always been more invigorating and inspiring than the dull ballast of scrupulous exactness.

That a law school is pre-eminently the proper place to learn law is the unquestioned judgment of this class. It has often been urged, with some apparent truth, that graduates of law schools are unable, upon their advent to the profession, to cope in practice with those adopting a different course. This is largely due to a lack of familiarity with the technicalities in procedure, and is of short duration. The newly organized Practice Court, in which this class is the pioneer, is designed to span this dreaded chasm between the legal tyro and the fully armed attorney. The technical part of any subject is a matter of easy acquisition to him who has laid a broad foundation in the fundamental principles of the science. But a law school is no royal road to legal knowledge, and can never supply the want of adaptability, diligence and industry.

The self-made man, that grand monument of human greatness, is usually noted by us after he has achieved success through long years of hard labor. Rarely do we stop to estimate the formidable obstacles he overcomes with the outlay of great mental energy, and never do we make a record of those who fall helplessly by the wayside in the vain effort to ascend the slippery heights of fame. Nothing is intended to disparage the laudable efforts of this individual. No words should be dropped except the sweet tokens of encouragement to those forced by circumstances to choose the longest course as the shortest way to reach their goal.

Confidence is the pilot of ability. It dares and does, while timidity begets failure. A thorough comprehension of the magnitude, the rough edges, sharp corners and smooth surfaces of a subject tends to prevent humiliating disappointment. It sounds timely warning of the ultimate effects of an apparently innocent shift in an adversary's line of battle. The wise principles inculcated at a law school rapidly ripen into practical experience, and lift from the pathway of the beginner many a cloud of despair and set the star of encouragement divinely there.

The present class saw one of the members of its Faculty distinguished by political preferment— elevated from the position of teaching law to the office of legislating national law. Such marked distinction found willing response in class patriotism and united action, without regard to party fealty or political affiliations, marked appropriately a well deserved honor. It is natural that students should take a just pride in the advancement of one of their leaders, but their rejoicing on this occasion was based on a broader and deeper foundation than mere personal choice. They had an abiding faith in his ability to make law from their actual knowledge of his ability to teach law. The ceremonies were well seasoned with that spirit and life so characteristic of the '94 law class, and the affair was conducted with such gratifying success that it can, in after years, be pointed to as a lasting tribute to the glorious achievements of the Law Department of the University of Michigan.

The juniors of '92 began their course with a change of professors in the chair of Domestic Relations and the Law of Wills, and it goes down as a matter of history in the class that the present incumbent of this chair has kept his end of the college table well supplied with ample food for reflection. And if there be a ninety-four law student so unfortunate as not to be thoroughly imbued with the value, with the trials and tribulations, of a searching quiz, perseverance and determination of purpose has in his case been a dismal failure.

The present year notes no abatement in the cultivation of forensic eloquence, and in many instances a marked improvement is perceptible. The Webster and Jeffersonian Debating Societies—transcendent bodies of their kind—descend to successive classes, like heirlooms, in perpetuation of instructive polemics. Each class brings eager recruits, willing to hazard failure that they may share the prowess of those departed. In these societies is generated an animating breeze to fan the dying embers of the well nigh lost art of speech making. Besides these debating societies there has been organized the Mechem, Griffin and Knowlton debating clubs, each composed of active members. The department has club courts galore, where the principles and knowledge gleaned in the lecture room and from books are practically applied.

The '94 Laws have their usual quota pursuing work in the Literary Department and will leave there enviable records of their fitness and skill. The present law class can boast of the most satisfactory relations with the Lits, that has for years existed between these departments. Only once, in a common cause, did they join in deadly combat, and on this occasion the Lits "lost their heads" and unceremoniously withdrew from the contest. But it never worries the Laws to see the Lits "lose their heads," since they couldn't possibly have any worse ones put on.

The Laws never neglect the proper cultivation of manly arts. They are this year well to the front in able competition for athletic honors. The average '94 Law has the general reputation of being able to jump higher, dive deeper and come out drier than any other element upon the campus.

Oratory has a peculiar charm for the law student. The present class is represented officially in the local Oratorical Association, and in all oratorical and debating contests some of its members have written their names on the dome of excellence.

In accordance with time honored custom, the Law Department this year lent its united strength in a becoming observance of Washington's Birthday. This day, of all others, is given up to the Laws. It is the day on which they are master of ceremonies and master of the situation.

Woman is well represented in the class of '94. However individual ideas may differ on this subject, it must be conceded that the time has arrived when the realm of thought must be unchained; when the unjust barriers to the progress of any class of persons, erected during barbaric times, must be completely overthrown. Lawyers of our early history were the first to lift their voices in defiance of the hirelings of tyranny, and sing the silver strains of personal liberty; and to the lawyers of to-day must be entrusted the full and proper application of those endearing principles. Lawyers must not wrap themselves in the burlap mantle of the past and sit shivering by the cold hearth-stone of mediaval intelligence. They must live in the present and look to the future.

There was a time in the history of English Jurisprudence when judicial tribunals of the highest character kneeled before the presumptive omnipotence of kingly curmudgeons, bowed before the power of haughty courtiers, and bent beneath the pressure of an opulent aristocracy. With the dawn of personal liberty the spirit of honor bright began to pervade the abode of justice. Indisputable as these facts may be, it is a rich gem in the crown of the noble profession of the law to know that judges were early placed on record as using their best directed efforts in securing the rights of man. Much has been accomplished through the arduous labors of untiring workers, yet there are broad fields of human interest still virgin to the plough share of modern civilization. The rich loam of human power mingled with the bones of sneering fossils will not yield its potency to the welfare of mankind until it has been turned up to the clear sun-light of reason.

The present class will leave the portals of this department in grateful recognition of the valuable services of the professors who are giving their lives and labors to an important work. Though some may escape in their native rusticity, the large majority have seized every available opportunity for advancement. The general tone and conduct of members of this class is an improvement on former years. They have shown a disposition to treat equals with charity, inferiors with magnanimity, and they have borne with pride the iniquity of being self-sustaining. So healthful has been this influence that many who were comparative strangers to diligent application have gradually emerged from the fog of listless slothfulness; have turned their backs to the withered husks of levity; and will graduate with their faces turned toward the rising sun of progress. ROBERT E. MINAHAN.

A Law Student's Dream.

IT is almost midnight. The beautiful college town is wrapped in a sweet silence, broken only by the tramp of some belated footman, or the mandolin song of some group of revellers.

The ponderous college clock strikes twelve with a slow and melancholy clang. It is the hour when all but owls, witches, and wizards should be nestled away in the soft lap of sleep. But yonder is a light gleaming through a window. Some student, perhaps, keeping his midnight vigils in his anxious search for the nuggets of truth and knowledge, and perchance in his mad career for fame.

It is Harry—a Law Student. With his head propped on his hand, he is intently poring over some tome of legal lore. He is said to be the best, though not the most brilliant, student in his class, and probably this midnight study tells us why.

But he lays aside the volume. Now he fixes his eyes upon a painting on the wall. It is of a middle-aged woman, calm, sweet, and beautiful, as a Madonna. The streaks of silver are just beginning to gleam through the raven black. Why, Harry, do you gaze so steadfastly? It is your mother.

Why do you take down that old album with the silver clasps? Why do you linger over the portrait of that old man whose locks are whitened with the frosts of winter? Why do you tarry over those girlish faces, and the portrait of that mischievous boy of ten? Ah, I have it! They are your father, sisters and brother.

What is this, Harry? Do not become flushed and confused. Tell me, what means this ringlet of golden hair? Why do you carry this miniature portrait of "Florence" in your watchcase? Your mind seems to wonder away. Is it over yonder in that little city that looks down into the blue waters of Lake Michigan? Is it there with that pure, trusting, golden-haired maiden, of nineteen summers? Harry, do you not fear, that in the hurry and bustle of the world, in the eager strife for fame and fortune, you will chill those warnings of the heart? I do not believe it.

What book is this, inscribed on the first blank leaf, "From father and mother." What words are you reading? I see: "Whatsoever ye would that men should do to you, do ye even so to them." But Harry, you cannot obey those noble words, and succeed in your chosen profession. He shakes his head reproachfully at this foolish advice.

Glancing again at the painting, the ringlet, and the portrait, Harry draws his luxurious, easy chair before the cheerful fire, and carelessly relaxes himself upon its cushions, intending to soothe his tired brain by calling up some of the spectres of the past, or framing, in his mind, some of the alluring phantoms of the future.

But scarcely had he seated himself, when sleep had closed his eyes, and Harry was in Dreamland. See the half-smile upon his countenance. He is dreaming sweet dreams; dreaming of the future—of events which, interwoven into the texture of his life, shall make it joyous and beautiful.

What a precious gift by our Maker, that when in dream we grope in the dim and shadowy To-Be, it springs into the flesh and blood of the Now. In Harry's dream, bright visions of his life, yet to be lived, were pictured as real and vivid as life itself.

These humble pages will sketch only those of his visions, which are the leading figures in the ideals of many a noble youth—who feels the hot blood leaping through his veins; who feels the lashings and spurrings of noblest ambition; who chafes and galls in his eagerness to take his place in the field of high action. And shall we omit the visions of the dear ones of the old home? Shall there not be some gentle spirit, of kindred sympathy, to smile away the frowns of misfortune, and to be the object of your thought and affection? Shall there not be deeds giving expression to your love of humanity?

These were the colors that gave beauty to Harry's bow of Hope.

In the first vision, Harry is established in his own law office in a large city, independent, if not yet prosperous. In his path are difficulties, but is Harry dismayed? Not he. Crushing defeats he may suffer, but he is now only learning the technique, by whish some day he will produce soul-stirring music, Already he has caught the eye of some of the great masters. He is known as an indefatigable worker, temperate, honest, and of bright promise. And is he not obeying that injunction we found him reading in the present "From father and mother?"

The vision shifts. Who will say that, aside from the conscious pleasure of duty done and lofty motive, Harry is not paid for his industry and uprightness? For, to-day, he is offered an interest in the business of the strongest law firm in the city. His answer to the offer you can readily guess. That plain little office is vacated, and Harry enters a larger field. An important branch of the business is put under his charge, and he controls and directs it with success and ability.

Now we see him addressing a jury, pleading for injured

innocence. His earnestness and sincerity give expression to an eloquence that moves and burns. The jury listen with bated breath—he has caught their sympathy! One more victory for Harry!

Again, we hear him arguing before the court. His honesty and clear argument, and the justice of his cause enlist the interest and favor of the judge. Another laurel for Harry!

Harry is fast ascending the steep path leading to that mount which is the goal of every lawyer's ambition, namely, Professional Eminence.

Those two years of struggle and success have not blunted Harry's finer feelings—affection for home and for Florence. He will soon see them all. To-day he leaves the city for a short absence. What genuine welcome! Father and mother receive him with tears of joy. Sisters and brother think him quite a hero. Harry is deeply touched by these tokens of love, and these unspoken praises, sweeter far than the acclamations of the great.

Once more Harry goes to the little city by the beautiful Lake Michigan. The golden ringlet and the little portrait, still treasured, tell the object of his coming. Again, Harry enters that familiar portal. It were better to draw a veil over that meeting. The scene is too holy for the curious eye of the world. Great joy is at the home of Florence to-day, for Harry has come.

In a few weeks Harry returns to the city, but not alone. By his side is the pretty, blushing Florence, now his wife.

He leads his bride to their own luxurious home. Their home life is simple and beautiful—filled with all those little acts and words and sacrifices, which bespeak perfect trust and sympathy.

Harry again plunges into the business of the office and the court, with greater energy than ever before. Life has a deeper meaning to him, and he no longer strives for Harry alone, but for Florence and Harry.

The years roll away and another vision rises in the dream. Harry has lived a life that has been pure and Godly. His fifty winters sit lightly upon him. Many have been his trials, many his struggles, but they only served to refine and ennoble —to drive away the dross, and leave behind the pure gold.

A lovely daughter and two kind, dutiful sons bring sunlight and gladness into the home of Harry and Florence. It is a joy to look into that home, the picture of peace and happiness, knowing no law but love.

Nor is his human sympathy dead. The years have only quickened it. His life is made beautiful by a deep, unselfish philanthropy, that seeks not the plaudits of the multitude.

Neither has he withdrawn from the world of action. He is ever in the thick of the fight. Long has he been the leading member of the firm, and the business has never fallen off. With years he has ripened in experience and wisdom.

He is a consummate orator, Many a forum is inspired by his magnetic presence; many a jury thrilled and electrified by his impassioned eloquence. He is acknowledged the greatest lawyer in the city. "A great and good man" is the common tribute. He is at the acme of his greatness. He has reached the goal—he has reached Professional Eminence.

"One!" strikes the college clock with a deafening clang Harry awakes with a start. He looks wildly about him, with a sad, troubled look. He presses his throbbing temples, and with voice tremulous with emotion, half regretfully mutters: "It was only a dream! Only a dream!"

VICTOR H. RINGER.

To "To Wit:"

FOND record of a long farewell,
Let rosemary and asphodel—
Those symbols that are known full well
To parting friends—
Their secrets on thy page reveal
And from the future sweetly steal
The thoughts that we would fain conceal
Till college ends.

For in the distant afterwhiles,
When we have travelled on for miles
Over Life's road with its tears and smiles,
The rosemary
Bids us remember this golden time
When Life ran smooth as a poets rhyme,
And seemed as sweet as a vesper chime
To revery.

In the battle of Life where'er we are,
Whether raised with its prizes or stamped with its scar,
Wherever we meet, in peace or in war,
The yellow and blue
Will call to our mind the tender scene
Of classmates and teachers and vistas green,
Whose classic walks of shadow and sheen
We've loitered through.

Full oft shall the festive banquet hall
Resound Ann Arbor's praise, and all
Our eloquence and songs shall call
Her mother dear.
When death shall claim us one by one,
(And some will rest ere the race is run),
Sweet tributes of praise to the silent one
Will be placed on his bier.

W. H. S.

Editorial.

THE editors of To Wit: have no hesitancy in launching another publication into the journalistic sea of the University of Michigan, for we feel that our Annual conflicts in no way with our contemporaries, and it is our aim to keep within our jurisdiction. Thus far in the history of the Department of Law no Annual of the nature of our own has ever been issued. We feel, therefore, that the time is ripe for such a publication, and that the class of ninety-four, which has been so active in other fields, is the class chosen for the introduction of a Law Annual to the University public.

As we had no precedent to guide us in our work, we have consulted freely with the faculty and those in a position to help us in regard to the book and its contents. To Wit: has but one sister-publication in this country, "The Shingle" of Yale Law School.

We are greatly indebted to our faculty advisory board, consisting of Professors Knowlton, Thompson and Mechem, as well as to Judge Thomas M. Cooley, President James B. Angell and Professor Johnson, for the great interest they have taken in our annual. To the remaining professors of the department the editors desire to express their appreciation for the many favors shown in the preparation of To Wit: The editors of To Wit: are especially indebted to the editors of the *Palladium* and *Castalian* for courtesies shown them. To the committees of the junior law class, George Konrath, G. B.

Dygert, W. C. Mand, we extend our thanks for their efforts in behalf of our publication, and to all of our friends who have given us encouragement and assistance we express our sincere thanks. To our publishers, The Register Publishing Company, the editors are grateful for many favors and courteous treatment.

The editors submit their finished work to the judgment of critical readers with a feeling that the present is but the first of many successive numbers of To Wit: Where we have left the work, our successors, we hope, will take it up and make this Annual of substantial value to the history of the Law Department.

Mr. Bryce, in his American Commonwealth, complimented the American universities on their liberal provisions for the scientific study of the law, and did us the honor to marvel at the high character and liberal culture of the professors who are engaged in giving this efficient instruction. Michigan has earned the full meed of this and other praise given to her law school, but not content with laurels already won, she is thinking of a new step in her progression—a move to a higher usefulness and a more commanding position among the law schools of the country. Ever watchful, and on the alert for ideas beneficial to herself and to her students, she recently sent a committee representative of the Regents and Faculty to visit the principal law schools in the East. After seeing the work done, and the good results of a three years course in other places, the committee reported themselves as favorable to a three years course here, and, although no action has been taken by the Board of Regents, the question is fairly launched and is being widely discussed by the students. The class of '94 is highly gratified that the subject is being mooted at this time, and hopes that the change will soon be made, for its advantages, although not directly shared by the class, will be material and lasting to both the school and the students. Competition in the legal profession was never so keen and bitter as it is to-day, and the necessity for a thorough equipment never so imperitive; add to this the fact that the trend of the different states is to an increase in the requirements for admission to the bar, and it will be apparent that the law schools must extend their law courses in order to prepare their students to successfully meet the increased rigidity of the bar examinations, and the fierce rivalry in the professional field. A three years course is far from being impracticable, as has been demonstrated by Harvard and Columbia in the East, and the University of California in the West, where the three years course has long since passed the experimental stage. Michigan must not lag behind, but instead, take her natural position in the forefront of American universities in this, as she has done in other departments. The two years' course now being offered is all that could be desired of a two years' curriculum, but a legal education should be more systematic, and less miscellaneous, than the best that can be given in so limited a time.

Besides the law work actually given, many advantages will accrue from a longer residence in a classical atmosphere, and from enlarged opportunities to do such work as is now done by the post-graduates, work so necessary to that cultured attainment which is a powerful auxiliary to the strengthening and perfecting of a lawyer's equipment. The additional year would insure more personal attention to the student from the professors, and more thorough work in many essential lines. A more extended study of text-books, supplementary to the lectures, could be given advantageously in some of the more important subjects that are now passed over with a short course of lectures; indeed, much of the first year could be devoted to laying a scientific basis for the lecture work, and the practical application of principles in the two succeeding years. The present course is broad enough, so all that is necessary to make it perfect is an additional year for a more exhaustive study. The Practice Court, which is hailed with delight by every student as a potent instrument for the making of practical lawyers, will be of incalculable benefit when used by the students during their second and third years. After three years text-book instruction, and lectures with a number of cases conducted through the Practice Court, no young man could hesitate a moment about relying upon his training for ultimate professional success.

The change would probably be marked at first, by a decrease in the number of students, but it would be for a short time only, for the corresponding increase in thoroughness and efficiency would attract to Michigan many men who now seek instruction elsewhere, and the reputation she would gain by the greater opportunities could not fail to fill her halls with aspiring young men.

The Class of '94 earnestly commends this change to the Regents, and hopes that they will see fit to adopt it in the near future.

THE poem entitled "Write a poem for TO WIT:" written by Mr. W. H. Kirk, is after the style of a similar poem by Youmans. Through a mistake part of the title of the poem was omitted. The title should read, "Write a Poem for TO WIT: *a la* Youmans."

In Memoriam.

William Gardiner Hammond.

ORGANIZATIONS

OFFICERS OF SENIOR CLASS.

Senior Class.

Class Colors—Red and White.

Class Yell.

Ki Yi, Ki Yi, Ki Yippi, Ki Yaw,
Michigan, Michigan, '94 Law.

Officers.

Robert Emmet Minahan, ...	*President.*
Augustus Asa Partlow, ...	*1st Vice-President.*
Miss Lulu Buffington Richardson, . .	*2nd Vice-President.*
Miss Emma Eaton, ...	*Secretary.*
George Frederick Zimmerman, . . .	*Treasurer.*
Victor Otho Coltrane, ...	*Valedictorian.*
Lott Russell Herrick, ...	*Historian.*
Daniel John Buckley, ...	*Prophet.*
Frank Crozier, ...	*Manager Field Sports.*
Julius Curtis Travis, ...	*Marshal.*
Daniel Heister Wingert, ...	*Assistant Marshal.*
Samuel McNeal Schall, ...	*Assistant Marshal.*

OFFICERS OF JUNIOR CLASS.

Junior Class.

Class Yell.

Ka Nock! Ka Nack! Ka-Niver, Ka-Naw!
Michigan, Michigan, '95 Law.

Officers.

William Albert Keerns, ...	*President.*
Francis Marion Talleson, ...	*1st Vice-President.*
Miss Agnes Frazier Watson, . . .	*2nd Vice-President.*
Charles Belknap Henderson, . . .	*Secretary.*
Warwick Miller Downing, ...	*Treasurer.*
Fred H. Gaston, ...	*Manager Field Sports.*
John Henry Simpson, ...	*Marshal.*
Quintin Amador Martinez, ...	*Assistant Marshal.*
George Abbey Salisbury, ...	*Assistant Marshal.*

Oratorical Association.

Officers.

J. H. Quarles,	*President.*
J. M. Davis,	*Vice-President.*
E. C. Lindlay,	*Secretary.*
H. R. Crozier,	*Treasurer.*
W. W. Wedemeyer,	*Delegate to Northern Oratorical Contest.*

Students' Lecture Association.

Officers.

J. W. Powers, Law, W. W. Wedemeyer, Lit,	*Presidents.*
S. C. Spitzer,	*Vice-President.*
W. C. McKinney, Dent, C. E. Wakefield, Lit,	*Corresponding Secty's.*
Frank H. Petrie,	*Recording Secretary.*
H. H. Whitten,	*Treasurer.*
C. K. Friedman,	*Assistant Treasurer.*
Miss Lucy E. Textor, Miss Lula B. Richardson,	*Committee.*

University of Michigan Athletic Association.

Officers.

HALBROOK G. CLEAVELAND,	*President.*
JOHN C. CONDON,	*Vice-President.*
A. C. CUMMER,	*Recording Secretary.*
EDMUND C. SHIELDS,	*Financial Secretary.*
EUGENE BATAVIA,	*Treasurer.*

Directors.

HOWARD E. CHICKERING,
W. P. MARTINDALE,
LOYD J. WENTWORTH,
JAMES BAIRD,
J. H. PRENTISS,
R. C. BOURLAND,
A. BLISS,
CHARLES C. MAC PHERRAN,
EDWARD C. WEEKS,
R. S. FREUND,
B. C. RICH,
L. B. LINDSLEY,
A. C. BARTELS.

'94 FOOT-BALL TEAM.

'94 Foot-Ball Team.

F. W. Ashton, *Manager.*

S. L. Avery, ...	*L. H. B.*
W. H. Burtner, ...	*Q. B.*
F. Crozier, ...	*L. E.*
H. L. Dyer, ...	*F. B.*
W. W. Holliday, ...	*R. E.*
O. J. Larson, ...	*R. T.*
W. H. L. McCourtie, ...	*L. G.*
J. L. Morrison, ...	*R. G.*
D. C. True, ...	*Center.*
A. Weinberg, ...	*L. T.*
L. C. Paul, Cap., ...	*R. H. B.*
H. E. Michael, ...	*Substitute.*
J. Newman, ...	*Substitute.*
J. H. Westcott, ...	*Substitute.*

'94 BASE-BALL TEAM.

'94 Base Ball Team.

Season of 1893.

J. KOENIGSTEIN,	*Catcher.*
R. G. SCOTT,	*Pitcher.*
J. L. MORRISON,	*1st base.*
W. V. ELLIOTT,	*2nd base.*
H. L. DYER,	*3rd base.*
W. W. PEPPLE, Capt.,	*Short stop.*
W. W. HOLLIDAY,	*Left field.*
W. W. WOODBURY,	*Center field.*
L. RINAKER,	*Right field.*
O. J. LARSON, Manager,	L. H. HANNA, *Substitute.*

Season of 1894.

J. KOENIGSTEIN,	*Catcher.*
R. G. SCOTT,	*Pitcher.*
J. L. MORRISON,	*1st base.*
W. V. ELLIOTT,	*2nd base.*
S. C. SPITZER,	*3rd base.*
W. W. PEPPLE,	*Short stop.*
W. W. HOLLIDAY, Capt.,	*Left field.*
W. W. WOODBURY,	*Center field.*
R. APPERSON,	*Right field.*
H. E. MICHAEL, Manager,	L. H. HANNA, *Substitute.*

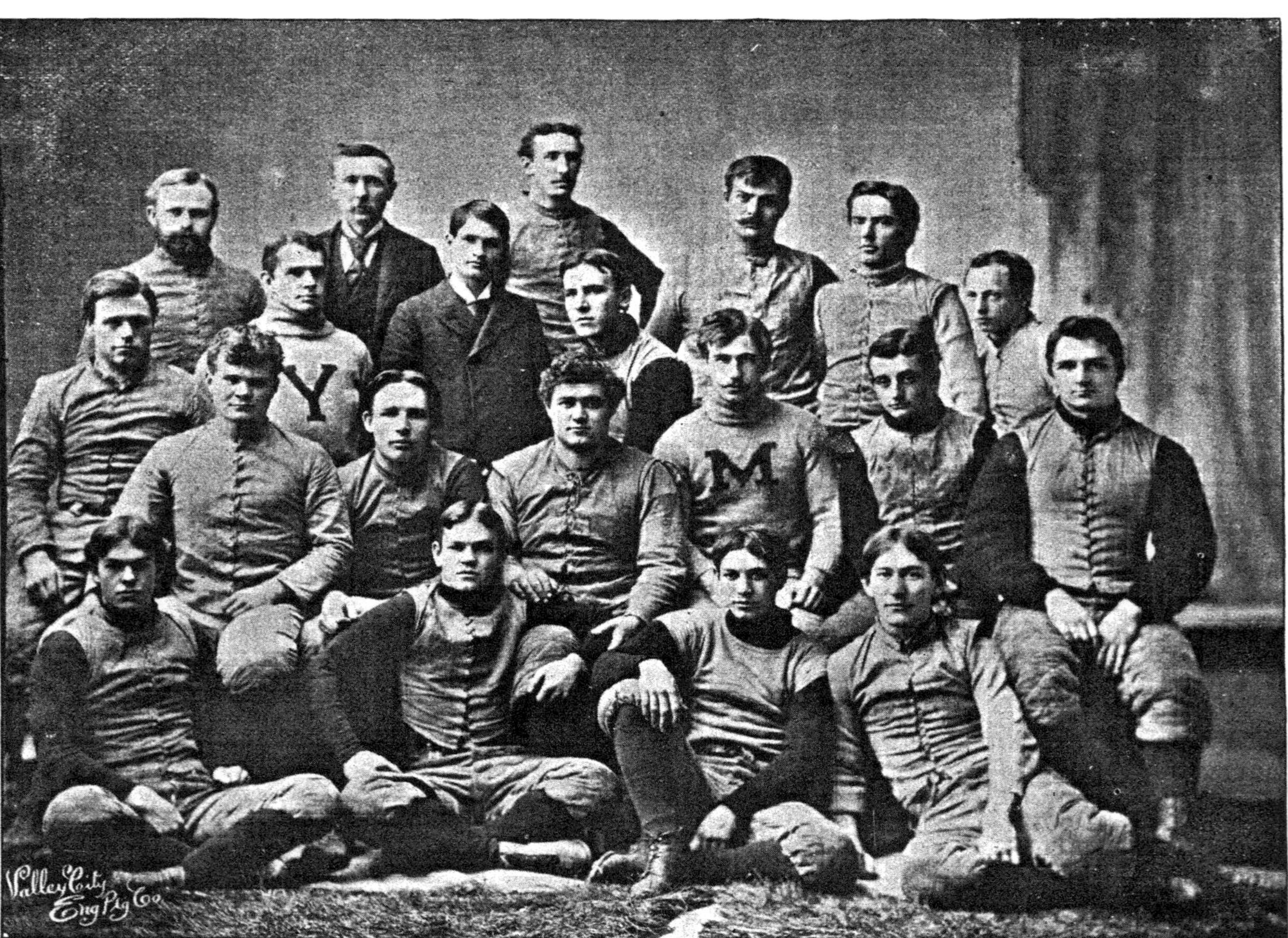
Valley City
Eng Ptg Co.

Varsity Foot-Ball Team.

Officers.

CHARLES BAIRD,	*Manager.*
EUGENE BATAVIA,	*Assistant Manager.*
GEORGE B. DYGERT,	*Captain.*
FRANK E. BARBOUR (Yale '91),	*Coach.*
ED. W. MOULTON,	*Trainer.*

Team.

Position	Name	AGE.	HEIGHT.	WEIGHT.
Ends	R. W. E. HAYES,	21	6 ft. 1½ in.	187
	H. M. SENTER,	20	5 " 11 "	157
	J. H. FERBERT,	20	5 " 7½ "	140
	ROGER SHERMAN,	21	5 " 7 "	145
Tackles	W. W. GRIFFIN,	25	5 " 8 "	175
	G. J. VILLA,	20	5 " 7 "	195
	W. I. ALDRICH,	21	5 " 10 "	175
	J. L. MORRISON,	22	5 " 11 "	170
Guards	J. HOOPER,	25	6 " 2½ "	210
	F. W. HENNINGER,	20	5 " 10½ "	175
Centers	C. H. SMITH,	20	5 " 10 "	230
	C. T. GRIFFIN,	24	5 " 9½ "	165
Quarters	JAMES BAIRD,	20	5 " 6 "	145
	GEORGE GREENLEAF,	19	5 " 6 "	130
Half-Backs	R. S. FREUND,	21	5 " 6½ "	134
	L. P. PAUL,	20	5 " 11 "	160
	A. C. BARTELS,	22	5 " 10 "	170
	L. C. GROSH,	22	5 " 9 "	150
	J. W. HOLLISTER,	23	5 " 8 "	163
	H. B. LEONARD,	21	5 " 8 "	155
Full-Backs	HORACE DYER,	23	5 " 11 "	175
	G. B. DYGERT (Captain),	23	5 " 4 "	160

Average weight of team,	177.
Average weight of line,	190.
Average weight of backs,	156½.
Total scores for Michigan,	272.
Average score per game,	27.
Total scores for opponents,	102.
Average score per game,	10.

Varsity Base-Ball Team.

Season of 1893.

Officers.

H. G. CLEAVELAND,	*Manager.*
FRANK CRAWFORD,	*Captain.*

Team.

FRANK CRAWFORD,	*Catcher.*
H. B. KROGMAN,	*Pitcher.*
A. W. JEFFERIS,	*1st base.*
E C. SPURNEY,	*2nd base.*
W. W. PEARSON,	*3rd base.*
S. C. SPITZER,	*Short stop.*
G. F. RICH,	*Left field.*
E. C. SHIELDS,	*Center field.*
C. B. SMELTZER.	*Right field.*

Substitutes.

R. E. RUSSELL, M. A. BANKS, T. P. GRIFFIN,
C. C. MAC PHERRAN.

Season of 1894.

G. J. CALDWELL,	*Manager.*
E. C. SHIELDS,	*Captain.*

Team for Southern Trip.

C. B. SMELTZER, RICHARD APPERSON,	*Catcher.*
J. W. HOLLISTER, H. B. KROGMAN,	*Pitcher.*
W. D. MCKENZIE,	*1st base.*
R. E. RUSSELL,	*2nd base.*
E. V. DEANS,	*3rd base.*
W. W. PEPPLE.	*Short stop.*
L. J. WENTWORTH,	*Left field.*
E. C. SHIELDS,	*Center field.*
G. W. BENTLY,	*Right field and pitcher.*

To Wit:

Published annually by the Senior Class of the Department of Law.

CHARLES A. DENISON, ... *Editor-in-Chief.*
EARL D. BABST, ... *Managing Editor.*
OREON E. SCOTT, ... *Business Manager.*
B. F. WOLLMAN, ... *Assistant Business Manager.*
FRANZ C. KUHN, ... *Assistant Business Manager.*

EDWIN W. SIMS, EUGENE BATAVIA, GEORGE W. FULLER,
HENRY C. WALTERS, CHARLES A. PARK.

Advisory Board.

PROF. J. C. KNOWLTON, PROF. B. M. THOMPSON,
PROF. F. R. MECHEM.

Michigan Law Journal.

Board of Editors.

RALPH STONE, ... *Managing Editor.*
HARRY D. JEWELL, ELI R. SUTTON.

University of Michigan Department.

E. J. JOHNSON, ... *Editor.*
H. C. WALTERS, ... *Assistant Editor.*

University Glee and Banjo Clubs.

Season of 1893-94.

Officers.

HARRY F. WORDEN, ... *President.*
SAMUEL MEDBURY, ... *Manager*, (resigned January).
B. S. VARIAN, ... *Manager*, (from January).

Executive Committee.

J. A. PRATT, H. F. WORDEN, J. B. TAYLOR,
W. W. WOODBURY. C. H. CONRAD.

Concerts.

Jackson,	South Bend,	Pontiac,
Lansing,	Cleveland,	Indianapolis,
Grand Rapids,	Toledo,	Louisville,
Chicago,	Detroit,	Dayton,
Cincinnati,	Flint,	Alpena,
Columbus,	Port Huron,	Bay City,
Saginaw,	Adrian,	Coldwater.

Glee Club.

J. A. PRATT, ... *Leader.*

First Tenor.	Second Tenor.
W. W. PEPPLE, '94,	J. A. PRATT, '94,
H. B. GAMMON, '94,	F. BRISCOE, '95,
A. W. REED, P. G.,	H. I. DUNTON, '96,
F. H. BURDICK, '96,	A. G. CUMMER, '96.
First Bass.	**Second Bass.**
A. J. PURDY, '94,	H. F. WORDEN, '94,
W. A. SPITZLEY, '95,	W. W. WOODBURY, '94,
C. MINER, '95,	C. E. MEAD, '96,
R. W. DUNN, '95,	B. F. McLOUTH, '95

Banjo Club.

J. B. TAYLOR, ... *Leader.*

Banjourines.	Banjos.
J. B. TAYLOR, '94,	A. TYROLER, '94,
H. E. SAUER, '96,	B. COLBURN, '95,
H. B. BODMAN, '96,	W. A. STARRETT, '97,
F. S. GERRISH, '97.	R. R. CASE, '95.

Mandolins.

R. D. EWING, '96,

J. S. PRATT, '96.

Guitars.

H. S. BARTON, '96,	C. H. CONRAD, '95,
H. W. CUMMINGS, '97.	C. H. MORSE, '95,

OFFICERS OF REPUBLICAN CLUB, 1893-4.

Republican Club.

Officers, 1893-94.

G. W. Fuller,	*President.*
E. W. Sims,	*Vice-President.*
A. A. Pearson,	*Recording Secretary.*
Harry Weinstein,	*Corresponding Secretary.*
H. F. Hussy,	*Treasurer.*

Executive Committee.

W. V. Elliott, J. J. Sheridan, A. W. Newton, L. G. Long, J. C. Travis, J. E. Swanger, C. A. Denison, E. D. Babst, C. S. Kingston, G. W. Fuller.

Officers, 1894-95.

J. J. Sheridan,	*President.*
H. M. Zimmerman,	*Vice-President.*
J. Q. Adams,	*Secretary.*
J. W. Dasef,	*Treasurer.*

Executive Committee.

G. W. Fuller, G. E. Leonard, F. C. Kuhn, C. A. Denison, L. O. Wadleigh, E. D. Babst, E. L. Allor, F. D. Adams, P. G. Burnham, H. F. Hussey, J. R. Arneill, A. J. Purdy, H. Weinstein.

OFFICERS OF DEMOCRATIC CLUB.

Democratic Club.

Officers.

A. E. McCabe,	*President.*
W. K. Moore,	*1st Vice-President.*
G. A. Everett,	*2nd Vice-President.*
C. A. McKnight,	*Corresponding Secretary.*
B. S. Gailey,	*Recording Secretary.*
F. B. Hamill,	*Treasurer.*
P. McGovern,	*Sergeant-at-Arms.*

Executive Committee.

Leonard Fisk, W. V. Moffett, C. P. Locke, L. B. Lindsay, H. D. Messick.

Prohibition Club.

Officers.

W. W. Mills,	*President,*
L. Hubbard,	*Vice-President,*
J. W. Looy,	*Secretary,*
H. L. Vorhees,	*Treasurer,*
F. N. Donaldson,	*Cor. Secretary.*

Cabinet.

M. L. Clawson,	*Law, V. P.,*
S. R. Cook,	*Lit, V. P.,*
C. Lahnis,	*Medic, V. P.,*
G. A. Parmenter,	*Dent., V. P.,*
L. Farnum,	*Pharmacy, V. P.*

Jeffersonian Society.

Officers from First of Year to Decemcer 13, 1894.

V. O Coltrane,	*President,*
J. L. Poston,	*Recording Secretary,*
H. D. Messick,	*Corresponding Secretary,*
A. G Mills,	*Critic,*
A. S. Reach,	*Treasurer,*
W. C. Hartman,	*Marshal.*

Officers from December 13, 1893 to February 8, 1894.

W. C. Hartman,	*President,*
A. L. Curtis,	*Vice-President,*
M. L. McLaughlin,	*Recording Secretary,*
C. E. Chadman,	*Corresponding Secretary,*
G. H, Kane,	*Critic,*
G. J. Geneback,	*Treasurer,*
O. E. Scott,	*Marshal.*

Present Officers.

A. S. Beach,	*President,*
C. E. Chadman,	*Vice-President,*
L. J. Eastin,	*Recording Secretary,*
R. N. McConnell,	*Corresponding Secretary,*
E. W. Marlatt,	*Critic,*
W. A. Coutts,	*Treasurer,*
W. C. Hartman,	*Marshal.*

NOT a Space Filler.

—*—*—*—

If you want to fill blank spaces on your upper shelves, it would be a mistake of judgement to buy the **Annotated Reprint of the New York Court of Appeals Reports** for that purpose. There are other legal works that will fill more space for less money, and to which no reference will ever be necessary. But if you want to get as many live authorities as possible in the least space on your working shelves, this edition of the most frequently cited of State Reports can hardly be improved upon **It is cheap**—being only $1 per original volume. **It is handsome**—being printed from new type.

Note This  

The space occupied by the first 100 volumes of editions now on market:

The Original Edition, Vols. 1 to 100, takes 14 feet, 2 in.
The Subscription Edition, 100 vols. in 50 books, takes 12 feet, 3 in.
The Annotated Reprint Edition, 100 vols. in 20 books, takes 4 feet.

And Note This 

FREEMAN P. LANE, of Lane & Briggs, Attorneys, 663-666, Bank of Minneapolis Building, Minneapolis, Minn., Nov. 23, 1893, says:—

You fail to *properly impress* on the minds of the legal fraternity the *value* and *importance* of the *annotations* There are no 100 books published that are as valuable to the *busy* lawyer. To illustrate, I had an important case come in *to-day*, involving the right of a railway company to use a public street without first compensating the adjoining owners. In five minutes I found the case of Story v. New York Elevated R R. Co., 90 N. Y. 122. The notes to that case alone will enable me to make more than the entire set costs. Every lawyer in the country should own a set.

And This  

From Hon. Stanley A. Smith, Judge of the Superior Court of California, in and for the County of Sierra.

The arrangement of the Reports is compact and convenient, both as to text and notes. The latter bears the impress of pains-taking care in their preparation, and are reliable.

And This  

From Michael A. Hartigan, Lawyer, Hastings, Neb., Nov. 21, 1893.

They are a great thing, and are to a person investigating the decisions of the Courts of New York, what the American Decisions are to the Courts of Last Resort for the first one hundred years of our Nation's Judicial History You can quote me as saying: That they are amongst the best books that a young man can put upon his shelves. *With the annotations they are equal to text books upon any subject covered by them.*

FOR TERMS AND OTHER INFORMATION, ADDRESS

H. B. PARSONS, Publisher,

105 Hudson Ave., ALBANY, N. Y.

Webster Society.

Officers, 1893-94.

First Semester.

F. E. Chamberlain,	*President,*
W. J. Landman,	*Vice-President,*
J. M. Adams,	*Secretary,*
L. Fiske,	*Treasurer,*
D. J. Edwards,	*Critic,*
H. T. Ronning,	*Marshal.*

Second Semester.

W. J. Landman,	*President,*
H. T. Ronning,	*Vice-President,*
H. M. Potter,	*Secretary,*
W. M. Downing,	*Treasurer,*
W. A. Keerns,	*Critic,*
F. E. Chamberlain,	*Marshal.*

Griffin Debating Club.

Officers and Members.

F. L. Anderson,
E. F. Clark, President,
J. H. Crowell,
H. A. Evans,
D. A. Edwards,
J. J. Harrington,
C. A. James, Secretary,
J. H. Lewman, Vice-President,
H. C. Mehan,
G. C. Maye,
E. W. Marlatt,
B. L. Oliver, President,
J. V. Pearson, President,
C. C. Stearns,
E. M. Wellman, President,
G. F. Zimmerman.

Mechem Debating Society.

Officers and Members.

E. W. Sims,	*President.*
F. W. Smith,	*Vice-Pres. and President.*
Oreon E. Scott,	*Treasurer.*
J. Z. Stewart,	*Vice-President.*
W. P. Harvey.	*Secretary.*
D. C. True,	*Vice-President.*
A. D. Bate,	*Secretary.*
J. E. Richardson,	*Treasurer.*
H. C. Walters,	*President.*
G. L. Reed,	*President.*
G. W. Phelps,	*Secretary.*

G. F. Waters, E. D. Pomeroy, A. S. Beach,
F. Walters, R. M. Ferguson, J. E. Barrell.
V. C. Coltrane, F. H. Hawthorn,

Columbian River Club Court.

Officers and Members.

A. S. Beach—Judge,
A. J. Bessie,
J. J. Bishop,
C. E. Cochran—Sheriff,
H. T. Condon—Clerk,
J. B. Dabney,
J. M. Davis,
T. J. Drumheller—Sheriff,
W. Isreal,
Q. A. Martinez,
G. W. Phelps—Judge,
C. H. Rector—Clerk,
G. L. Reed,
L. L. Stevens—Judge,
W. H. Smiley,
H. C. Vidal—Judge,
J. H. Westcott—Judge,
J. B. Wright—Sheriff.

A Perfect Equipment for the Searcher for Authorities.

The American Digest	IN THE	American Digest Holder.

A library may hold many text books and reports, yet, if it lacks the American Digest, it is incomplete, and may fail the man who depends upon it at the time of need. Text books grow out of date. Reports are full of overruled cases. The latest decision of the court is what counts as authority.

The American Digest,

(7 VOLUMES,)

Covers the entire case law of the past seven years, including

The Last 120,000 Cases,

Fully and accurately digested, intelligibly classified, and, by means of the most ingenious mechanical and typographical contrivances, **made available** for the quickest examination by the busy lawyer.

With the U. S. Digest added on the lower shelves, (as shown in the picture,) all the rest of the American case law will be within reach in digest form.

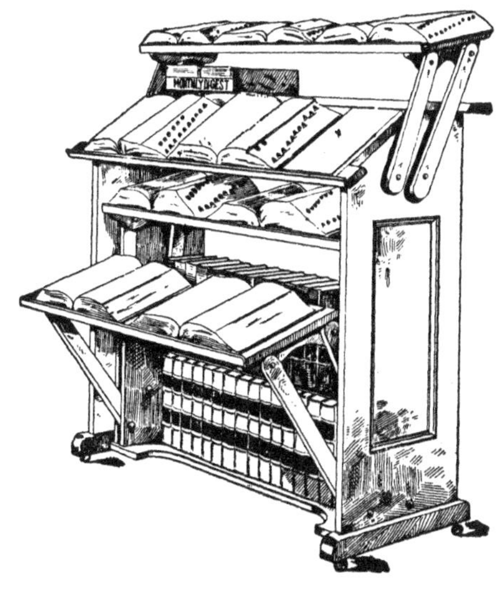

WRITE FOR PARTICULARS TO

WEST PUBLISHING CO., St. Paul, Minn.,

Publishers of Text Books, Reports, and Digests.

Dealers in New and Second-Hand Law Books.

N. B. Catalogues and Sample Copies of the Reporters Sent on Request.

California Club Court.

Officers and Members.

G. W. Bentley—Justice of Peace,
F. G. Crothers—Judge,
C. B. Henderson—Justice,
H. B. Howe—Judge,
F. Hauke—Justice of Peace,
T. Ludlow—Clerk,
J. P. Mahon—Judge,
E. C. Owens—Judge,
M. L. Tyner—Judge.
M. L. Coleman—Attorney,
W. Downing—Sheriff,
W. Hervey—Attorney,
J. J. Ingle—Judge,
W. H. Kirk—Atty. and Court Poet.
L E. Mahon—Judge,
B. L. Oliver—Superior Judge,
M. L. Sullivan—Clerk,

Empire Club Court.

Officers and Members.

H. B. Anderson—Sheriff,
J. M. Adams—Clerk,
M. L. Coleman,
John Davis,
R. L Ewbank,
W. S. Flint,
G. W. Fuller,
Frank Garrett,
H. B. Howe,
J. H. Miller,
L. J. Neun,
J. W. Powers—Judge,
Miss L. B. Richardson,
L. L. Redich,
J. V. I. Rosencrans,
E. R. Shoecraft,
L. O. Wadleigh.

Pennsylvania Club Court.

Officers and Members.

G. L. Glitsch—Clerk,
R. A. Hitchens,
W. H. Leahey,
E. W. Marlatt—Judge,
J. M. Mohney—Judge,
S. M. Schall—Sheriff,
W. R. Thirkield,
J. T. Wagner—Sheriff,
Geo. V. McConahey,
A. L. Lehman,
Wm. Coults,
H. J. Makiver,
J. H. Hassinger—Judge,
T. S. Lackey,
J. B. Luce,
H. A. Miller—Clerk,
V. A. Powell—Judge,
J. H. W. Simson—Sheriff,
J. P. Volk,
H. H. Patterson—Pros. Attorney,
Chas. Showalter—Clerk,
Agnes A. Watson,
S. H. Hoverter,
J. H. Crowell.

Canadian Club.

Officers.

First Semester.

Norman B. Price, Lit, ... *President,*
Mrs. J. E. Pettigrew, Medic, ... *Vice-Presidens,*
Frank Walters, Law, ... *Secretary,*
J. R. Le Touzel, Medic, ... *Marshal.*

Second Semester.

Henry C. Walters, Law, ... *President,*
Mrs. J. E. Pettigrew, Medic, ... *Vice-President.*
G. R. Stone, Law, ... *Secretary,*
J. R. Le Touzel, Medic, ... *Marshal.*

Ohio Club Court.

Officers and Members.

Seniors.

Fred W. Ashton,
George H. Bailey,
Richard L. Cameron,
Charles E. Chadman,
Ralph Hartzell,
Charles H. Mattingly,
Robert S. Parks—Judge,
John W. Zuber,
Charles F. Adams,
Milton L. Clawson,
John C. Cole,
Ulysses G. Denman,
William B. Locke,
Homer D. Messick—Judge,
Louis P. Paul,
Wm H. Burtner.

Juniors.

George H. Cushing,
H. C. De Rau,
George A. Everrett,
James W. Harter,
Jonas E. Kindleigh,
Ralph C. Lovering,
Charles L. McDowell,
Claud Sheldon,
Sanford G. Baker,
Walter R. Clayton,
Walter M. Ellett,
Frederick J. Flagg,
Richard K. Jones,
George Konrath,
Fredrick E. Matson—Clerk,
Andrew R. Nichols,
Stanley A Reese,
Philo G. Burnham,
Leward L. Redick.

Nebraska and Iowa Club Court.

Officers and Members.

G. L. Bowman,
F. G. Clark—Judge,
T. W. Day—Judge,
J. W. Ferrier,
F. H. Gaston,
J. J. Harrington,
W. G. Hoover,
C. F. Kimball,
W. A. Koenigstein,
A. M. Lewald,
F. W. Marsh,
W. K. Moore—Clerk,
J. V. Pearson,
C. A. Plank,
E. M. Wellman,
C. A. Bull,
Miss Emma Eaton—Judge,
W. A. Eckels—Judge,
B. Friend,
W. W. Goodykoontz,
J. E. Haddock,
K. W. Hunt,
J. Koenigstein,
C. H. Kubat,
G. E. Leonard,
W. H. Merner,
C. H. Paul,
C. A. Pratt—Clerk,
S. F. Reece,
A. W. Wier.

Utah Club Court.

Officers and Members.

Geo. Halverson—Judge,
H. S. Harris,
J. T. McGregor,
J. J. McClellan, Jr.—Clerk,
E. C. Robinson,
N. J. Harris,
J. A. Harris,
J. H. McDonald,
Jos. E. Page—Clerk,
J. Z. Stewart—Sheriff.

Michigan Club Court.

Officers and Members.

E. L. Allor,
M. M. Atherton,
E. W. Atwood,
G. H. Bayliss,
C. R. Bishop,
C. A. Brayton,
B. F. Bunting—Chief Justice,
F. E. Chamberlain—Pros. Atty.,
J. F. Chambers,
W. A. Cannon,
O. B. Conant,
W. A. Cook,
F. C. Cook,
H. R. Crozier,
F. Dewis,
C. F. Donahoe,
D. A. Edwards,
G. M. Evans,
R. M. Ferguson—Sheriff,
I. Foster,
G. A. Garner,
O. C. Garret,
G. J. Genebach,
A. P. Gilmour,
J. W. Gillespie,
C. L. Goodwin,
E. B. Goss,
W. P. Harvey—Associate Justice,
J. M. Harvey,
J. L. Hollander,
W. P. Honey,
M. J. Howard,
J. F. Henry,
H. R. Jewet,
J. J. Kiley,
F. C. Kuhn,
W. J. Landman—Associate Justice,
O. J. Larson,
E. F. LeGendre,
H. P. Lewis,
C. P. Locke—Clerk,
H. J. McKay,
M. L. McLaughlin,
W. W. Mills,
A. Mosher,
W. H. Murray,
J. J. Noon,
V. J. Obenauer,
T. L. O'Brien,
M. O'Connor,
W. H. Padley,
L. R. Palmer,
E. J. Parker,
J. L. Pearl,
W. Pierpont,
D. Porter,
C. A. Park,
B. F. Reed,
H. G. Reek,
J. E. Richardson,
H. E. Root,
G. A. Salisbury,
W. B. Seely,
J. J. Sheridan,
E. W. Sims—Pros. Atty.,
F. W. Smith,
C. A. Stearns,
H. L. Stearns,
I. A. Thoren—Sheriff,
D. C. True—Chief Justice,
J. J. Vlach—Clerk,
J. D. Wakely,
H. C. Walters,
F. Walters,
B. Wiley,
E. H. Wetzel—Treasurer,
H. M. Zimmerman.

Kansas Club Court.

Officers and Members.

E. B. Baker,
A. G. Burr,
A. J. Curran,
E. A. Hafner—Clerk,
S. A. Jetmore,
J. H. Mays,
H. E. Michael,
W. F. Miller—Sheriff,
M. S. Rice—Sheriff,
J. J. Vlack—Judge,
C. W. Burch—Judge,
Grant Conklin,
Frank Garrett—Clerk,
O. E. Hopkins—Judge,
I. B. Lipson,
R. N. McConnell—Judge,
W. C. Michaels—Sheriff,
D. C. Reeves,
J. C. Tobias—Sheriff,
J. G. Wine—Clerk.

Missouri Club Court.

Officers and Members.

J. W. Bingham—Clerk,
Wm. Dobbins—Sheriff,
J. T. Hays—Sheriff,
J. W. Kimberlin,
R. L. Motley—Judge,
D. C. Reeves—Sheriff,
H. C. Smith—Judge,
J. E. Swanger—Judge,
J H. Westcott,
V. O. Coltrane—Pros. Atty.,
L. J. Eastin—Clerk,
R. J. Kirkpatrick,
H. C. Livengood—Clerk,
W. O. McNary—Clerk,
G. B. Rosenburg,
E. Spalding,
M. Westover,
T. M. Tollison.

Indiana Club Court.

Officers and Members.

Ned Abercrombie,
C. C. Bishop,
Geo. F. Felts—Judge,
W. C. Mand,
J. H. Cotner,
M. E. Fitzgerald,
Melvin Leliter,
Henry T. Ronning,
J. C. Moore,
F. M. Springer,
W W. Pepple,
C. L. DeVault—Pros. Attorney,
Frank H. Dunnahoo,
John Meteer,
Edward McCulloch,
G. W. P. Brown,
M. M. Bruce—Clerk,
W. A. Keerns,
V. H. Ringer,
Lyman Jones,
C. H. Tindall,
W. S. Sykes,
S. L. Strinkle,
W. W. Holliday,
W. C. Hartman—Jus. Supr. Court,
C. D. Orear—Judge,
L. A. Shane,
G. F. Zimerman—Judge, Clerk,
E. C. C. Henning,
Chas. Fitzgerald,
C. C. Stearns,
James Taylor—Sheriff,
Frank Crozier,
L. A. Stoneman,
Z. Taylor,
Roy H. Williams.

Illinois Club Court.

Officers and Members.

G. J. Arbeiter,
F. L. Anderson,
R. J. Barr,
Walter S. Carr,
Chas. D. Cary,
Bert H. Cockett—Clerk,
O. E. Cramer,
Martin J. Dilleore,
Jesse L. Deck—Sheriff,
States Dickson,
Geo. W. Dayton,
H. A. Evans—Sheriff,
V. O. Ford,
J. W. Ferrier,
R. L. Gunter,
Lucien Gray,
V. A. Gerenger,
W. J. Galbraith,
Jesse Heylin,
F. B. Hamill,
Lott R. Herrick—Asso. Justice,
Richard K. Jones,
C. A. James,
Otto Kaspar,
Roy J. Kirkpatrick,
John H. Lewman—Chief Justice,
Allen G. Mills,
E. W. Morris—Clerk,
Q. A. Martinez,
W. W. North,
Louis T. Orr—Clerk,
A. A. Partlow—Chief Justice,
C. E. Pope,
H. M. Porter,
A. A. Reiss,
G. L. Reed—Associate Justice,
M. H. Scott,
Geo. H. Simpson,
Albert C. Salter,
Walter B. Strang,
Arthur J. Vinson—Sheriff,
Chas. E. Ward,
Geo. T. Wells,
S. D. Weil,
A. Weinberg—Sheriff.

Representative Alumni.

Gresham M. Barber, '60, 10 Wick Block, Cleveland, Ohio.
John Graves, '60, U. S. Court Room, Detroit Mich.
Mason D. Chatterton, '61, Attorney-at-Law, Lansing, Mich.
Noah W. Cheever, '65, 10 N. Fourth Ave., Ann Arbor, Mich.
Levi L. Barber, '65, 30-31 Buhl Block, Detroit, Mich.
James L. High, '66, 103 Adams St., Chicago, Ill.
Job Barnard, '67, 500 5th St., Washington, D. C.
Marshall D. Ewell, '68, 613-14 Ashland Block, Chicago, Ill.
John F. Lawrence, '68, Opera House Block, Ann Arbor, Mich.
Julius G. Pomerne, '68, 521 Society for Savings Bldg., Cleveland, Ohio.
Oscar J. Campbell, '70, Society for Savings Bldg., Cleveland, Ohio.
Rufus H. Thayer, '70, Atlantic Bldg , Washington, D. C.
Oliver H. Dean, '71, Kansas City Nat'l. Bank Bldg., Kansas City, Mo.
Emerson H. Eggleston, '71, 50 Euclid Ave., Cleveland, Ohio.
Amos Denison, '72, 34 Blackstone Bldg., Cleveland, Ohio.
A. W. Martin, '73, 711 Tacoma Bldg , Chicago, Ill.
Fred. A. Maynard, '76, 1 and 2 New Houseman Block, Grand Rapids, Mich.
Donald McPherson, '77, Attorney-at-Law, Washington, D. C.
Henry Wollman, '78, Wales Building, Kansas City, Mo.
Theodore M. Bates, '79, Board of Equalization and Assessment, Cleveland, Ohio.
Gustav A. Laubscher, '79, 531 Society for Savings Bldg., Cleveland, Ohio.
B. W. Viers, '81, 112 W. Washington St., Chicago, Ill.
Walter H. Hughes, '82, 21 Morris Bldg , Grand Rapids, Mich.
Samuel C. Blake, '83, 504-5 Society for Savings Bldg., Cleveland, Ohio.
Arthur C. Denison, '83, Michigan Trust Co. Bldg., Grand Rapids, Mich.
John M. Core, '85, 29 E Main St., Uniontown, Pa.
Thomas D. Kearney, '85, W. Huron St., Ann Arbor, Mich.
Charles O. Smedley, '85, Attorney-at-Law, Grand Rapids, Mich.
Roger M. Lee, '86, Perry-Payne Bldg., Cleveland, Ohio.
Thomas A. Bogle, '88, Masonic Block, Ann Arbor, Mich.
Amzi W. Strong, '88, 1111 Ashland Block, Chicago, Ill.

Nicholas P. Whelan, '88, 605 Society for Savings Bldg., Cleveland, Ohio.
J. Q. Copeman, '90, Attorney-at-Law, Ashland, Wis.
Seth W. Knight, '90, Attorney-at-Law, Mt. Clemens, Mich.
W. W. Meloan, '90, Attorney-at-Law, Macomb, Ill.
Frank M. Sheridan, '90, 1006 N. Y. Life Bldg, Kansas City, Mo.
Geo. A. Katzenberger, '90, 48 Reaper Bldg., Chicago, Ill.
J. D. Wendorff, '90, 842 N. Y. Life Bldg., Kansas City, Mo.
W. H. Churchill, '91, 60–61 Sentinel Bldg., Milwaukee, Wis.
John Dwan, '91, County and City Attorney, Two Harbors, Mich.
Frederick A. Henry, '91, 113 Superior St., Cleveland, Ohio.
Duncan G. Inverarity, '91, 100–6 Occidental Bldg., Seattle, Wash.
Harry D. Jewell, '91, Register of Probate, Grand Rapids, Mich.
Geo. S. Johnson, '91, 703 Oriel Bldg., St. Louis, Mo.
William Kaufman, '91, 86–88 Bakewell Bldg., Pittsburg, Pa.
Chas. E. Sweet, '91, Prosecuting Attorney for Cass County, Dowagiac, Mich.
Hugh E. Wilson, '91, Widdecomb Bldg., Grand Rapids, Mich.
William P. Bourland, '92, City Hall, Kansas City, Mo.
Harrison B. McGraw, '92, 808 Perry-Payne Bldg., Cleveland, Ohio.
Benjamin Parmley, Jr., '92, Cuyahoga Bldg., Cleveland, Ohio.
Ralph Stone, '92, The Mich. Trust Co. Bldg., Grand Rapids, Mich.
Kirk E. Wicks, '92, 3 Old Houseman Bldg., Grand Rapids, Mich.
Genit H. Albers, '93, over Nat'l. City Bank, Grand Rapids, Mich.
Ulysses V. Bickley, '93, Attorney-at-Law, Hamilton, Ohio.
William J. Conroy, '93, N. Y. Life Bldg., Omaho. Neb.
Henry W. Jarvis, '93, 1623 Curtis St., Denver, Col.
Gelmer Kuiper, '93, 1025 Mich. Trust Bldg., Grand Rapids, Mich.
John A. Rooney, '93, Attorney-at-Law, Nebraska City, Neb.
H. A. Reese, '93, Attorney-at-Law, Lincoln, Neb.
John A. Titsworth, '93, Attorney-at-Law, Rushville, Ind.

Junior Class.

List of Members.

NAME.	RESIDENCE.
Michael Barnett Aaron,	Chicago, Ill.
Charles Francis Abbott, A. B., *Dartmouth College*,	Gardner, Mass.
Frank DeForest Adams,	Marshall, Mich.
Robert Milligan Addleman,	Zollarsville, Pa.
Elmer Louis Allor, B. S., *Univ. of Mich.*	Mt. Clemens, Mich.
Henry Boardman Anderson,	Chateaugay, N. Y.
George John Arbeiter, B. L., *University of Illinois*,	Ann Arbor, Mich.
Marvin Melville Atherton,	Sparta, Mich.
Edwin Wood Atwood,	Flint, Mich.
George Emerson Bailey,	Hillsdale, Mich.
Sanford Garlcome Baker, B. S., *Northern Indiana University*,	Woodville, O.
Frank Warren Ballenger,	Flint, Mich.
Richard James Barr,	Wilton Centre, Ill.
Arthur Calvin Bartels,	Denver, Col.
George Howard Bayliss, B. S., *Northern Indiana Normal University*,	Hudson, Mich.
James Beach Beckett, Ph. B., *Yale University*,	Chicago, Ill.
Greeley Whitlaw Bently,	Los Angeles, Cal.
James Harvey Bigger,	Allegheny, Pa.
William Stock Bigger,	Allegheny, Pa.
John William Bingham,	Milan, Mo.
Herman Aurelius Birkhead, B. S., *West Kentucky College*,	Ensor, Ky.
Claude Corbly Bishop, B. S., *National Normal University*,	Walton, Ind.
Jonathan James Bishop,	Port Townsend, Wash.
Henry Blatchford, A. B., *McGill University*,	Chicago, Ill.
George Lowden Bowman,	LeMars, Ia.
Claude Arthur Brayton,	Howell, Mich.
George Washington Peritory Brown,	Mt. Vernon, Ind.
Emory Durward Brownlee,	Kingfisher, O. T.
Harry Conant Bulkley, A. B., *Univ. of Mich.*	Monroe, Mich.
John Sidney Burnet,	Chicago, Ill.
Philo G. Burnham, B. S., *Antioch College*,	Woodstock, O.
Nellie Bunn Burke,	Atlanta, Ill.
Alex Bernard Bush, A. B., *Detroit College*,	Detroit, Mich.
Norman McLaren Cameron,	Denver, Col.
Arthur Delancy Campbell,	Ann Arbor, Mich.

OVER

Name	Residence
Guilford Elvene Campbell,	Vandalia, Mich.
William Austin Cannon,	Washington, Mich.
Walter Scott Carr,	Argenta, Ill.
Charles Edwin Carter,	California, Pa.
Ira Randolph Carter,	Oxford Junction, Ia.
Charles David Cary,	Rantoul, Ill.
Llewellyn Barton Case,	Utica, N. Y.
Lemuel Oliver Caswell,	Bozeman, Mon.
Walter Roy Clayton,	Troy, O.
Bret Harte Cockett,	Joliet, Ill.
Daniel Martin Cook,	Williamston, Mich.
Frank Christopher Cook,	Detroit, Mich.
Wirt Arthur Cook,	Saline, Mich.
James Allen Cotner,	Logansport, Ind.
William Alex Coutts,	Pilot Mound, Manitoba.
Arthur Howe Covert, A. B., *Univ. of Mich.*	Ann Arbor, Mich.
Robert Byron Crane,	Kalamazoo, Mich.
Lee Randall Crawford,	Colebrook, N. H.
Hubert Richmond Crozier,	Ann Arbor, Mich.
Andrew Judge Curran, B. S., *Kansas Normal College*,	Cherokee, Kan.
Charles Wesley Curtis,	West Sumpter, Mich.
Henry Howard Cushing,	Toledo, O.
John Nelson Davis,	Roseburg, Ore.
George William Dayton,	Gainesville, Tex.
Jesse LeRoy Deck,	Roodhouse, Ill.
H. Clifton De Ran, B. S., A. B., *National Normal University*,	Old Fort, O.
Charles Lemuel DeVault,	Churubusco, Ind.
Otis Franklin Dickey,	Rigdon, Ind.
States Dickson, B. S., *Lombard University*,	Kewanee, Ill.
Thornton Dixon,	Dundee, Mich.
William Dobbins,	Arkoe, Mo.
Walter Dohany,	Farmington, Mich.
Cornelius Francis Donahoe,	Ishpeming, Mich.
Warwick Miller Downing,	Denver, Col.
Thomas Francis Doyle,	LaSalle, Ill.
Thomas Jesse Drumheller,	Walla Walla, Wash.
William Gray Duncan,	Dunbar, Pa.
Robert Winfield Dunn,	Chicago, Ill.
Harry Irving Dunton,	Canandaigua, N. Y.
Paul Dillingham Durant,	Columbus, Ill.
George Burlingame Dygert, Ph. B., *U. of M.*	Ann Arbor, Mich.
Charles Wesley Eastman,	Menominee, Mich.
Frank Lewis Edinborough,	West Bay City, Mich.
George Collinwood Edwards,	Houghton, Mich.
Walter Millard Ellett, Ph. B., *Mt. Union College*,	Alliance, O.
Evan Lawrence Evans,	Corunna, Mich.
George Adams Everett, B. S., *Fayette Normal University*,	Lytton, O.
Richard Lazenby Ewbank,	Guilford, Ind.
John William Ferrier,	Council Bluffs, Ia.
Maurice Elmer Fitzgerald,	Logansport, Ind.
Frederick Junius Flagg	Toledo, O.
Walter Scott Flint,	Potsdam, N. Y.
George Edward Foerster,	Lansing, Mich.

Vernon Okey Ford	Chicago. Ill.
Isaac Foster, ...	Gladwin, Mich.
Frank Garrett, A. B., *Hamilton College*, .	Leavenworth, Kan.
Fred H. Gaston, B. S., *Highland Park Normal College*, ...	Martinsburg, Ia.
Curtis Frank Gilkey, ...	Plainwell, Mich.
John Wilber Gillespie, ...	Denver, Col.
Allan Pegram Gilmour, A. B., *University of Virginia*	Henderson, Ky.
George Luther Glitsch.	Johnstown, Pa.
Clayton Spencer Goodwin, ...	Ann Arbor, Mich.
William Ward Goodykoontz, ...	Boone. Ia.
Thomas Peter Grace, ...	St. Paul, Minn.
Lucien Gray	Lewistown, Ill.
Robert Lee Gunter, A. B., *Newbeiry College*,	Wagener, S C.
Harry Graydon Hadden, ...	Englewood, Ill.
Edward August Hafner, B. L., *Central College*, ...	Enterprise, Kan.
Roy Faris Hall, ...	Tuscola, Ill.
Fred Benner Hamill, ...	Homer, Ill.
Edward Thomas Hamilton	Dallas, Tex.
James William Harter, ...	Osceola, O.
George William Harvey, ...	Escanaba, Mich.
Thomas Scott Hayden, Jr., ...	Denver, Col.
John Thomas Hays, ...	Republic, Mo.
Charles Belknap Henderson, ...	Elko, Nev.
Leo Kilian Hennes, A. B., *Detroit College*,	Detroit, Mich.
John Frederick Henry, ...	Brooklyn, Mich.
Jesse Heylin, ...	Canton, Ill.
Charles Frederick Hille, ...	Alma Centre, Wis.
Richard Allen Hitchens, ...	McKeesport, Pa.
Willis Edwin Hodgman, ...	Coldwater, Mich.
John Willis Hollister, A.B., *Williams College*,	Cambridge, N. Y.
William George Hoover, ...	Blue Hill, Neb.
Horace Banfill Hord, ...	Indianapolis, Ind.
Edward Horsky	Helena, Mon.
Moulton Jones Hosack, ...	Scottdale, Pa.
Matthew Joseph Howard, ...	Iosco, Mich.
Schuyler Colfax Hubbell, ...	Goshen. Ind.
Philip Sawyer Hudson, ...	Ann Arbor, Mich.
Harry Herbert Hunt	Chicago, Ill.
Kay William Hunt, B. S., *Drake University*,	South Omaha, Neb.
Jerome Ingersoll, ...	Detroit Mich.
Emil Benjamin Isgreen, ...	Ogden City, Utah.
William Israel, ...	Helena, Mon.
Howard Alfred Jackson	West Middlesex, Pa.
Samuel Abraham Jetmore, ...	Marion, Kan.
Henry Root Jewell, ...	Adrian, Mich.
John Lyman Jones, ...	Mapleton. Ind.
Roland King Jones, ...	Akron, O.
Otto Kasper, ...	Chicago, Ill.
Frank Kauke, B. S., *Northern Indiana Normal University*, ...	Macedonia, Ia.
William Albert Keerns, B. S., *Central Indiana Normal University*: . . .	Clinton, Ind.
Jonas E. Kendeigh, ...	North Amherst, O.
Charles Dean Kennedy	Ann Arbor, Mich.

Joseph Wesley Kimberlin, ...	Kansas City, Mo.
Roy Judson Kirkpatrick, ...	St. Louis, Mo.
Benjamin Killey Knight	Santa Cruz, Cal.
Will August Koenigstein, ...	Norfolk, Neb.
George Konrath, Jr., ...	Erastus, O.
Thomas Stevens Lackey, ...	Allegheny, Pa.
Rufus Gillett Lathrop, A. B., *Univ. of Mich.*	Detroit, Mich.
William Henry Leahy, ...	Pittsburg, Pa.
Albert Lincoln Lehman, ...	Lashley, Pa.
Melvin E. Leliter, ...	Rolling Prairie, Ind.
Linley Grant Long	Quaker City. O.
Ralph Courtney Lovering, ...	Findlay, O.
Israel Ludlow, ...	Los Angeles, Cal.
Arthur Lussky, ...	Chicago, Ill.
James Patrick Mahan, ...	Blue Lake, Cal.
Lawrence Edward Mahan, ...	Blue Lake, Cal.
Harry Jacob Makiver, Ph. B., *Lafayette Coll.*,	Russellville, Pa.
Walter Clifford Mand, ...	Terre Haute, Ind.
Guy Clay Mars, ...	Berrien Springs, Mich.
Meredith Read Marshall, ...	Allegheny, Pa.
Quintin Amador Martinez, ...	Penasco, New Mexico.
Frederick Eugene Matson, B. S., *Muskingum College*, ...	Duncan's Falls, O.
James Henry Mays, ...	Ann Arbor, Mich.
George Van Vorhis McConahey, . . .	Claysville, Pa.
Edward Martin McCulloch, B. S., *Wabash College*, ...	New Albany, Ind.
Charles Sumner McDowell, ...	Canton, O.
Peter McGovern, Jr., ...	Sherburn, Minn.
Henry J. McKay, ...	Romeo, Mich.
Richard Matthew McMahon, ...	Chicago, Ill.
William Oscar McNary, B. S., *Tarkio College*, ...	Tarkio, Mo.
John Meteer, A. B., *Wabash College*, .	Grand River, Indian Ter.
William Clopton Michaels, ...	Holton, Kan.
Harvey Alvin Miller, B. S., *Grove City College*, ...	Apollo, Pa.
William Frederick Miller, ...	Paola, Kan.
Wiley Wright Mills, A. B., *Hope College*, .	Brooklyn, Mich.
Joseph W. Mitchell, ...	Beacon, Mich.
Will Hudson Mitchell, ...	Fulton, Ill.
Elmer William Moore, ...	Braddock, Pa.
Edgar William Morris, B. L., *University of Illinois*, ...	Onarga, Ill.
William Ernest Murphy, ...	Greenville, Tex.
William Hanson Murray, ...	Milan, Mich.
Louis James Neun, ...	Rochester, N. Y.
Jacob Bernard Nockels, ...	Carroll, Ia.
James Joseph Noon, ...	Michigan Centre.
William Warren North, ...	Lockport, Ill.
George Edwin Noyes, ...	Gorham, N. H.
Victor John Obenauer, A. B., *Olivet College*, B. S., *Olivet College*, ...	Detroit, Mich.
Marr O'Connor, ...	Detroit, Mich.
Walter Joseph O'Donnell, ...	Pittsburg, Pa.
Louis Thomas Orr, ...	Kankakee, Ill.
Gottfried Fred Ottmar, ...	Ann Arbor, Mich.

James Veech Oxtoby,	Ionia, Mich.
William Henry Padley,	Pinckney, Mich.
Harry Hemphill Parsons.	Missoula, Mon.
John Evander Patton,	Chattanooga, Tenn.
Charles Howard Paul,	St. Paul, Neb.
James Harvey Payne,	McKeesport, Pa.
John S. Pearl,	Belleville, Mich.
Charles Phillips,	California, Pa.
Warren Pierpont,	Owosso, Mich.
Henry Moses Porter, A. B., *Atlanta University*,	Aiken, S. C.
Frank Quintus Quinn,	Saginaw, West Side.
Leonard Le Roy Redick,	Mansfield, O.
Sanford Levi F. Reece,	Union, Ia.
Henry George Reek, B. S., *Central Normal College*,	Custer, Mich.
Stanley Alfred Rees, B. S., *National Normal University*,	Red Lion, O.
David Calvert Reeves,	Tarkio, Mo.
Merton Stacher Rice, B.S., *Baker Univevsity*,	Baldwin, Kan.
Alfred Drury Riess,	Red Bud, Ill.
Ross Morrell Rininger,	Stoyestown, Pa.
†Ezra Clark Robinson,	Farmington, Utah.
Edward Sidney Rogers,	Orchard Lake, Mich.
Glenn Beal Roseberry,	Maryville, Mo.
Joe Van Inwegen Rosencranse,	Sing Sing, N. Y.
Warren Scott Rundell,	Mayville, Mich.
George Abbey Salisbury,	Ann Arbor, Mich.
Albert Charles Salter,	Englewood, Ill.
Obadiah Sands, Jr.,	Chicago, Ill.
Marmion Hilton Scott,	Kempton, Ill.
Henry Edward Albert Siefried,	Chicago, Ill.
Lewis Shackleford,	Lexington, Ky.
Perry A. Shanor, A. M., *Thiel College*,	McKeesport, Pa.
Claud Ebenezer Sheldon, Ph. B., *Hiram College*,	Windham, O.
Almond Gould Shepard,	Shepardsville, Mich.
Ernest Russell Shoecraft,	Ann Arbor, Mich.
Charles McDonald Showalter,	Oxford, Pa.
George Henry Simpson,	Englewood, Ill.
John Henry Simpson,	Dravosburg, Pa.
William Hudson Smiley,	Spokane, Wash.
William Morris Smith,	Bath, Mich.
Newton Carmen Spencer,	Linden, Mich.
Jacob Steketee,	Grand Rapids, Mich.
Alexander Stewart,	Rock Island, Ill.
Edwin Hollis Storie,	Chariton, Ia.
Walter Benjamin Strang,	Roodhouse, Ill.
Heber Truman Strong,	Detroit, Mich.
Martin Lewis Sullivan,	Stockton, Cal.
Francis Marion Talleson, Ph. B., *Searcy Coll.*,	Ozark, Ark.
Zachary Taylor,	Fort Branch, Ind.
Wilbur Roscoe Thirkield,	Monongahela, Pa.
William Harold Thompson,	Alexandria, Minn.
Theodore Axel Thoren,	Negaunee, Mich.
Warren Wesley Travis,	La Porte, Ind.
Horace Tupper, Jr.,	Bay City, Mich.

Daniel Francis Turney, ...	Caledonia, N. Y.
Melvin LaMont Tyner, ...	Salem, Ia.
Emmet Pitt Updergraff, ...	Panora, Ia.
Willison Kerr Vance, ...	Monongahela, Pa.
Raymond Elmoine Van Syckle, B. S., *Univ. of Mich.*	Bay City, Mich.
Albani Joseph Violette, ...	Missoula, Mon.
Joseph Peter Vlk, ...	Allegheny, Pa.
Harry Rowen Wair	La Porte, Ind.
Arthur John Waldron;	Pueblo, Col.
Walter Scott Wall, ...	La Porte, Ind.
Thomas Moore Wallace	Lewistown, Pa.
Winfred James Wallace, ...	Ypsilanti, Mich.
Edward Marion Walsh;	Oakland, Cal.
Agnes Fraser Watson, ...	Allegheny, Pa.
Elbert Alexander Watson, ...	Detroit, Mich.
William Walter Wedemeyer,	Chelsea, Mich.
Simon D. Weil, ...	Chicago, Ill.
George Fitch Wells, ...	Garner, Ia.
Frank Anton Wenter, ...	Chicago, Ill.
Myron Westover, ...	St. Louis, Mo.
Ernest Henry Wetzel, ...	Saginaw, East Side.
General Grant White, ...	Lena, O.
William Kihnie Whitfield, ...	Sullivan, Ill.
Guy Joseph Wicksall, ...	Bangor, Mich.
Adolphus William Wier	Heppner, O.
Roy Hughes Williams, ...	Milan; O.
Jacob Good Wine, ...	Harrington, Kan.
Judd Winton, ...	Centreville, Pa.
Henry James Witbeck.	Chicago, Ill.
Roger Irving Wykes, ...	South Grand Rapids.
Henry Martin Zimmermah	Marine City, Mich.

Special Students.

NAME.	RESIDENCE.
Fritz Edgar Anderson;	Rockland, Mich.
Nathan Davis Corbin, M S., ...	Ann Arbor, Mich.
Thomas L. O'Brien, ...	Alma, Mich.
LeRoy Palmer, ...	Coldwater, Mich.
Will Barney Seeley, ...	Evart. Mich
Francis Adams Stivers.	Liberty, Ind.
William Shipp Withers, B. L., *Cumberland University*	Hopkinsville, Ky.

The students named below, enrolled in the Department of Literature, Science, and the Arts, also pursue studies in the Department of Law:

Thomas Parks Bradfield, ...	Grand Rapids, Mich.
George Jason Cadwell, ...	Chicago, Ill.
William Herbert Charnley, ...	Goshen, Ind
Robert Victor Friedman, ...	Muskegon, Mich.
Robert Foote Hall, ...	Williamston, Mich.
Ray Hart, ...	Midland, Mich.
Jesse Cameron Moore	Delphi, Ind.
Edgar Martin Morsman, Jr.;	Omaha, Neb.
Frederick Whittlesey Newton, . . .	Saginaw, East Side, Mich.
Roger Sherman, ...	Chicago, Ill.